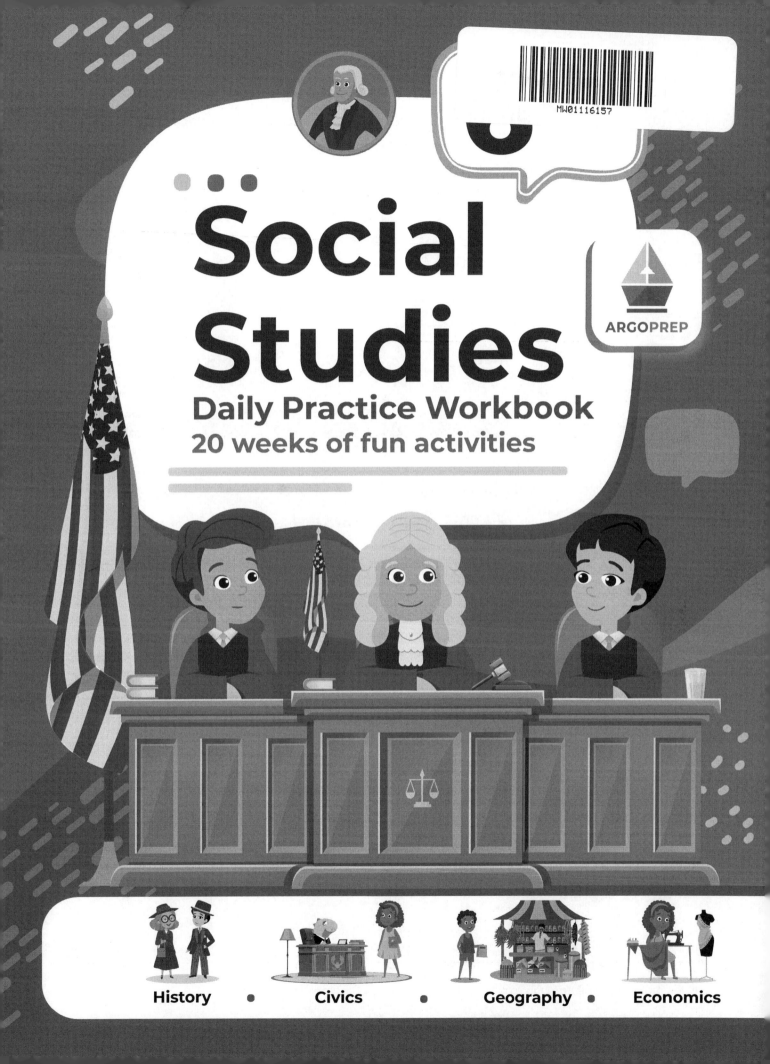

# Social Studies

**Daily Practice Workbook**

20 weeks of fun activities

ARGOPREP

History · Civics · Geography · Economics

ArgoPrep is one of the leading providers of supplemental educational products and services. We offer affordable and effective test prep solutions to educators, parents and students. Learning should be fun and easy! To access more resources visit us at www.argoprep.com.

Our goal is to make your life easier, so let us know how we can help you by e-mailing us at: info@argoprep.com.

- ArgoPrep is a recipient of the prestigious **Mom's Choice Award**.

- ArgoPrep also received the 2019 **Seal of Approval** from Homeschool.com for our award-winning workbooks.

- ArgoPrep was awarded the 2019 **National Parenting Products Award, Gold Medal Parent's Choice Award** and **the Tillywig Brain Child Award.**

# SOCIAL STUDIES

Social Studies Daily Practice Workbook by ArgoPrep allows students to build foundational skills and review concepts. Our workbooks explore social studies topics in depth with ArgoPrep's 5 E's to build social studies mastery.

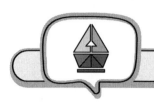
# Introduction

Welcome to our six grade social studies workbook!

This workbook has been specifically designed to help students build mastery of foundational social studies skills that are taught in six grade. Included are 20 weeks of comprehensive instruction covering the four branches of social studies: History, Economics, Civics, and Geography.

# Table of Contents

# How to Use the Book

All 20 weeks of daily activity pages in this book follow the same weekly structure. Students will work through each week with ArgoPrep's 5 E's to build mastery on the topic: **Engaging, Exploring, Explaining, Experiencing,** and **Elaborating** on the topic.

The activities in each of the sections align to the recommendations of the National Council for the Social Studies which will help prepare students for state standardized assessments. While the sections can be completed in any order, it is important to complete each week within the section in chronological order since the skills often build upon one another.

Each week focuses on one specific topic within the section. More information about the weekly structure can be found in the Weekly Planner section. This workbook also comes included with detailed video explanations which you can find on our website at argoprep.com/social6.

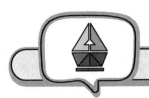
## Weekly Planner

| Day | Activity | Description |
|---|---|---|
| 1 | Engaging with the Topic | Read a short text on the topic and answer multiple choice questions. |
| 2 | Exploring the Topic | Interact with the topic on a deeper level by collecting, analyzing and interpreting information. |
| 3 | Explaining the Topic | Make sense of the topic by explaining and beginning to draw conclusions about information. |
| 4 | Experiencing the Topic | Investigate the topic by making real-life connections. |
| 5 | Elaborating on the Topic | Reflect on the topic and use all information learned to draw conclusions and evaluate results. |

## How to access video explanations?

Go to **argoprep.com/social6** OR scan the QR Code:

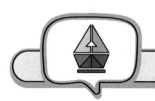

# List of Topics

| Unit | Week | Topic |
|---|---|---|
| Geography & Civilization | 1 | Day 1. Political Geography<br>Day 2. Physical Geography<br>Day 3. Population & Agriculture<br>Day 4. Oceans & Deserts<br>Day 5. Challenges & Adaptations |
| Neolithic/Agricultural Revolution | 2 | Day 1. From Paleolithic to Neolithic<br>Day 2. Domestication<br>Day 3. Benefits & Challenges of Agriculture<br>Day 4. Social Structure<br>Day 5. Neolithic Revolution: Good or Bad? |
| Mesopotamia & Egypt | 3 | Day 1. Geography & Climate<br>Day 2. Government & Writing Systems<br>Day 3. Religious Beliefs<br>Day 4. Law & Justice<br>Day 5. Technological Advancements |
| Indus River Valley | 4 | Day 1. Geography & Climate<br>Day 2. Archaeology, Anthropology, & History<br>Day 3. Urban Planning & Infrastructure<br>Day 4. Characteristics of Culture<br>Day 5. Effects of Climate Change |
| Yellow River, China | 5 | Day 1. Geography & Climate<br>Day 2. Timelines & Chinese Dynasties<br>Day 3. Mandate of Heaven<br>Day 4. Confucianism & Harmony<br>Day 5. Chinese Writing System |

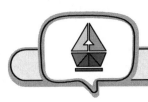
| Unit | Week | Topic |
|------|------|-------|
| Religions of East and South Asia | 6 | Day 1. Hinduism & Confucianism<br>Day 2. Buddhism & Sikhism<br>Day 3. Comparing Eastern Religions<br>Day 4. Analyzing the Spread of Buddhism<br>Day 5. Respecting Sacred Ideas, Objects, and Places |
| Religions of Southwest Asia and Europe | 7 | Day 1. Judaism & Zoroastrianism<br>Day 2. Christianity & Islam<br>Day 3. Comparing Religious Beliefs<br>Day 4. Centuries and the Spread of Christianity<br>Day 5. Tourism & Sacred Sites |
| Chinese Civilizations - Qin & Han | 8 | Day 1. Basics - Qin & Han Dynasties<br>Day 2. Government & Legal Systems<br>Day 3. The Great Wall of China<br>Day 4. Achievements of the Qin and Han<br>Day 5. Exploring Human Nature |
| Mediterranean Civilizations: Ancient Greece | 9 | Day 1. Ancient Greece - Athens & Sparta<br>Day 2. Ancient Greece - Alexander the Great & the Hellenistic Era<br>Day 3. Greek Direct Democracy<br>Day 4. Roots of Academic Language<br>Day 5. Greek Gods & Goddesses |
| Mediterranean Civilizations - Ancient Rome | 10 | Day 1. Origins of Rome<br>Day 2. Spread of the Roman Empire<br>Day 3. Roman Monumental Architecture<br>Day 4. Roman Representative Democracy<br>Day 5. Rome and Christianity |

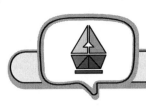

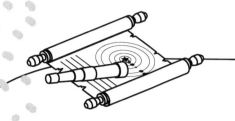

# WEEK 1

# Geography & Civilization

This week you will learn about the basics of geography, such as understanding a map and a compass rose, as well as ways in which humans interact with different environments around the world.

ARGOPREP

**Directions:** Use the map to answer the following questions.

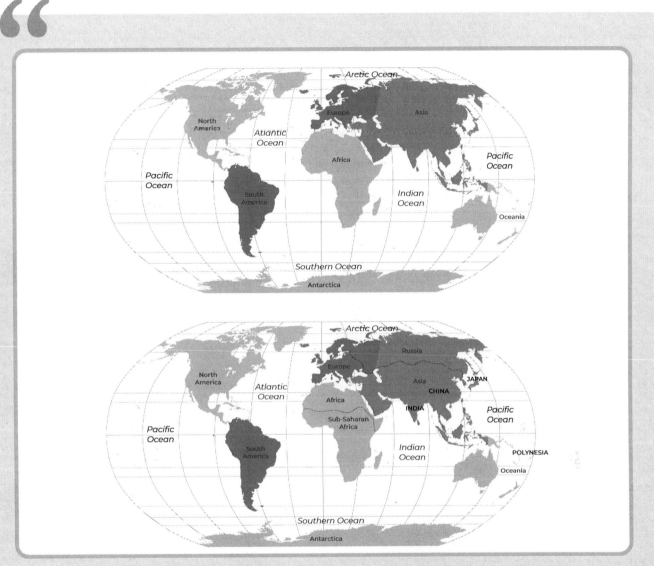

The Eastern Hemisphere is where we find the continents of Asia, Oceania, Africa, and Europe. There are many different countries and cultures within each **region**. Regions are areas of land where the people share a common culture, climate, or other characteristic. To help you learn where things are in the Eastern Hemisphere, it is important to know the **cardinal and intermediate directions**. The **cardinal directions** are north, east, south, and west. You can find these labeled on the **compass rose**. The **intermediate directions** are between the cardinal directions. Northeast is between north and east. Southeast is between south and east. Northwest and southwest follow the same pattern. See if you can find each of the cardinal and intermediate directions on the compass rose!

1. Which of the following best describes the purpose of the Compass Rose?

    **A.** It shows where north, east, south, and west are located on the map.

    **B.** It provides information about distance from one place to another.

    **C.** It helps determine which direction the sun is traveling.

    **D.** It provides your current location on the map.

2. If you are in Russia and want to go to India, in which direction should you travel?

    **A.** North          **B.** East          **C.** South          **D.** West

3. To get from Europe to Central Asia, in which direction should you travel?

    **A.** North          **B.** East          **C.** South          **D.** West

4. What direction should you travel to get from Sub-Saharan Africa to China?

    **A.** Northeast          **B.** Southeast          **C.** Northwest          **D.** Southwest

5. Japan is ............................................................ of Polynesia.

    **A.** Northeast          **C.** Northwest

    **B.** Southeast          **D.** Southwest

**Directions:** Find the compass rose on the map below and fill in the cardinal and intermediate directions.

In order for humans to thrive and populations to grow, they need access to two very important things: food and fresh water! Throughout history, communities have developed along rivers, coastlines, and in areas with good farming. For the next two weeks, you will be focusing on some of the early **river valley civilizations**. Even though they developed thousands of years ago, they continue to have an impact on today. Some of the major population centers today are located near those ancient civilizations! The major **population clusters** of the ancient world were located in East Asia along the Yellow and Yangtze rivers, in South Asia along the Indus River, and in Northeastern Africa along the Nile River. Another major population cluster was along the Tigris and Euphrates rivers in southwestern Asia.

**Directions:** Use the map to answer the following questions:

1. Find the compass rose and label the cardinal and intermediate directions. Use the map from Day 1 to check your work.

2. In what region will you find the Yellow River?

   **A.** Sub-Saharan Africa          **C.** South Asia

   **B.** East Asia                         **D.** Southeast Asia

3. In what region will you find the Nile River?

   **A.** Polynesia                        **C.** Central Asia

   **B.** Eastern Europe               **D.** Northeastern Africa

4. Which two rivers are the closest to each other?

   **A.** Tigris River and Euphrates River

   **B.** Nile River and Euphrates River

   **C.** Yangtze River and Indus River

   **D.** Indus River and Yellow River

5. The Mediterranean Sea separates which two continents?............................................

   ..................................................................................................................................

6. The root word sub means "under" or "below." Use this information to describe the location of "Sub-Saharan Africa."............................................................................

   ..................................................................................................................................

**Directions:** Read the text below. Then answer the questions that follow.

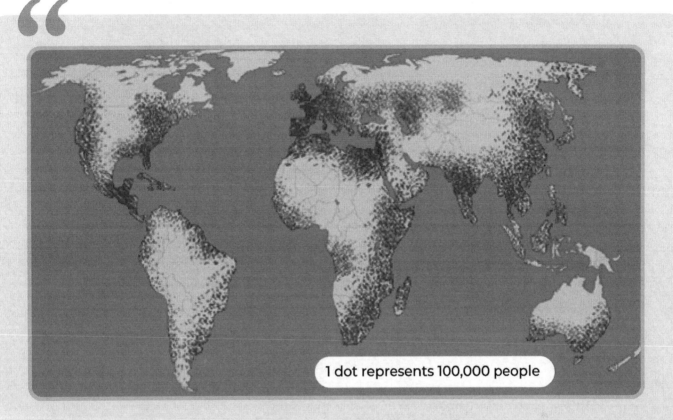

1 dot represents 100,000 people

**Population density** is a measure of how many people live within a certain area (often per square mile or square kilometer). A **dot distribution map** shows population density by using a dot that represents a certain number of people within a specific area. The map above shows that each dot represents 100,000 people. With this type of map, we can clearly see that some of the largest population clusters are along rivers, such as the Yangtze and Yellow rivers.

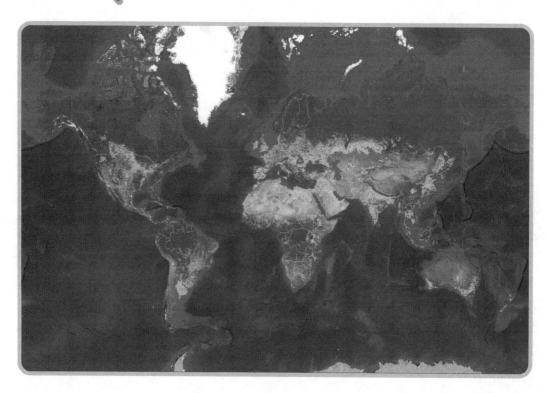

You learned on Day 2 that access to fresh water is very important. The other requirement is food! The process of growing food is called **agriculture**. Agriculture is one of the main ways that people around the world get their food, and you will learn more about it in Week 2. The map above shows the location of farms all around the world. To answer the questions below, you will need to use the maps from today's lesson as well as days 1 and 2.

**1.** In what part of Asia will you find the fewest people? ..............................................

**2.** Why is there so little farming to the west of the Nile River?

........................................................................................................................

**3.** Which two rivers are in the same region as the major population clusters of East Asia?

    **A.** Tigris R. & Euphrates R.

    **B.** Tigris R. & Nile R.

    **C.** Indus R. & Yangtze R.

    **D.** Yangtze R. & Yellow R.

"

On Day 3 you learned about the importance of agriculture to provide food for growing populations. But not all areas of the Earth are good for growing food! People who live in deserts or on islands are able to thrive as well, they just need to use different techniques.

Many deserts have small areas with access to fresh water, usually from an underground source called an **aquifer**. An area with fresh water in a desert is called an oasis. A community will often develop around an **oasis**. Nomadic groups travel from one oasis to another, bringing goods and information with them. These **pastoral nomads** live in the desert and rely on the products from their animals for food, clothing, and shelter. They trade these goods for items that they can not produce, such as fresh vegetables and fruit. Pastoral nomads also share information and news that they have gathered on their travels. By relying on oasis networks and their own skills, pastoral nomads developed ways to live in the desert.

People who live in island environments often have limited space for farming. For them, the ocean is the source of much of their food. Fish, clams, crab, and other animals make up a large portion of their diet. Seaweed and other marine plants are also very important. Some communities practice **aquaculture**, which is kind of like "fish farming!" By caring for and maintaining clam beds, or by building rock enclosures that trap fish and wash away waste, island communities have developed many ways to maintain the ocean as a food source.

Fresh water can also be a scarce resource for islanders. Some communities are able to capture and save rainwater. Others, however, rely on other methods. Many islands contain natural underground aquifers where seawater has been heavily filtered into drinkable freshwater. These aquifers can sometimes have a spring near the coastline. With careful use, these water sources can support growing populations.

"

"

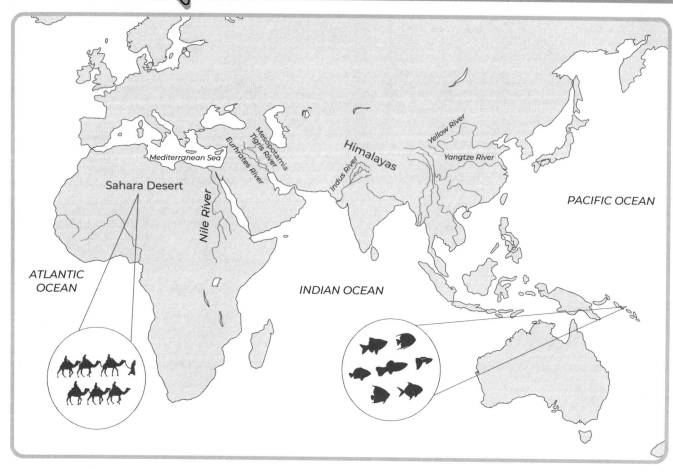

**Directions:** After reading the passages above, respond to the following prompt:

**1.** What unique challenges do people in desert and island environments face in getting enough food and water to support larger populations?

.............................................................................................................................

.............................................................................................................................

.............................................................................................................................

.............................................................................................................................

.............................................................................................................................

.............................................................................................................................

.............................................................................................................................

.............................................................................................................................

.............................................................................................................................

.............................................................................................................................

**Directions:** This week you learned about three different environments and how people in those areas obtain food and water. Fill in the chart below to show what you've learned.

|  | Agricultural Communities | Desert Pastoral Nomads | Island/Ocean Communities |
|---|---|---|---|
| **How did they get food?** |  |  |  |
| **How did they get water?** |  |  |  |

People in each of these environments have developed ways to obtain food and water. But imagine if those systems stopped working!

1. Describe how you think people might react if their water and food resources are limited for at least one year?

..................................................................................................................................................

..................................................................................................................................................

..................................................................................................................................................

..................................................................................................................................................

..................................................................................................................................................

2. What if they struggle to find food and water for longer than a year? What might they do to continue surviving?

..................................................................................................................................................

..................................................................................................................................................

..................................................................................................................................................

..................................................................................................................................................

..................................................................................................................................................

..................................................................................................................................................

Throughout history, humans have developed new technologies to deal with changes in access to food and water. Read about each technological advancement in the map below.

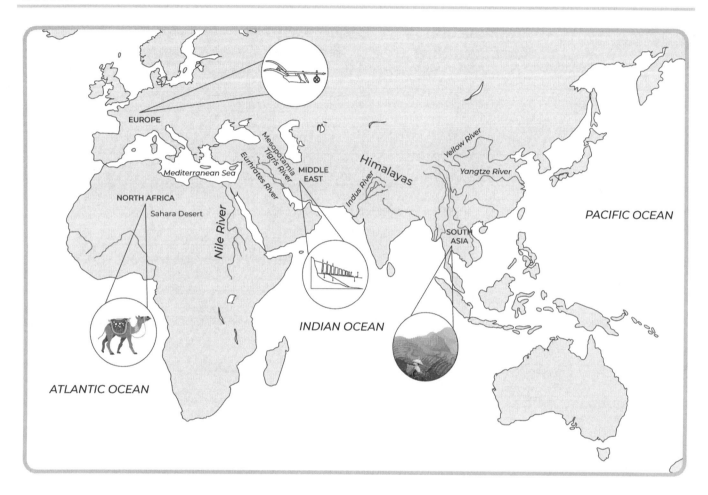

**The heavy plow**: The soil of Northern Europe was thick and heavy. After the heavy plow (or plough) was introduced, agricultural production quickly increased and more people could be fed!

**Qanat system**: Water can quickly evaporate in the hot desert climate. To more efficiently move water from mountain aquifers to the cities, the Persians developed the qanat: man-made "rivers" that moved water underground for hundreds of miles. By transporting water underground, they were able to limit evaporation!

**Terracing**: In areas with heavy rainfall and steep hillsides, the healthy topsoil and seeds can be washed away. By forming the hillside into giant "steps," farmers could grow crops on the flat portion while keeping the water where they needed it!

**Camel saddle:** Nomadic groups rely on trade to get food. The camel saddle was developed to make it easier to ride and pack a camel for longer journeys.

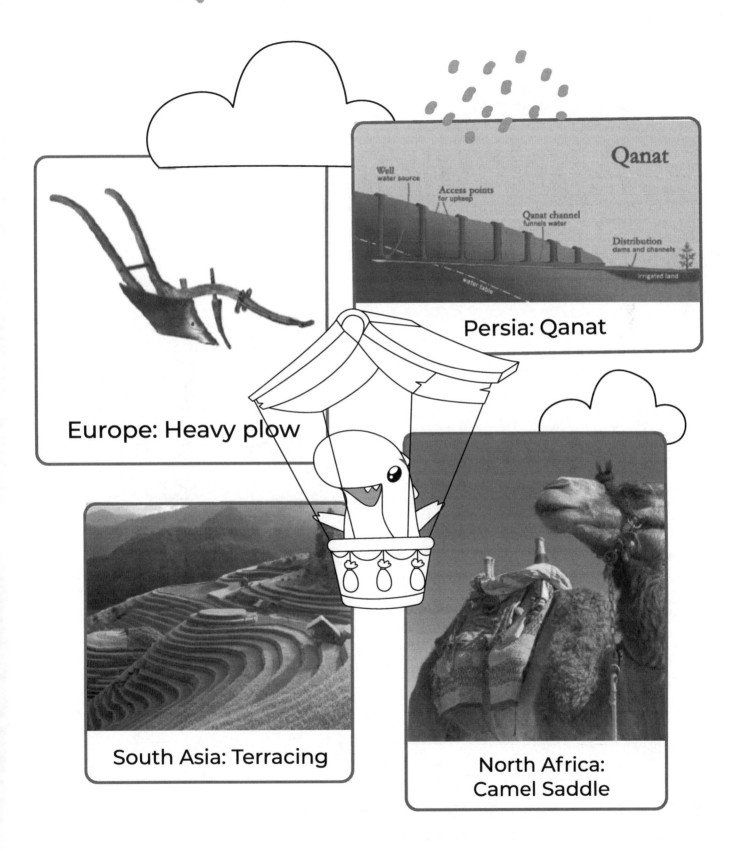

Europe: Heavy plow

Persia: Qanat

South Asia: Terracing

North Africa: Camel Saddle

# WEEK 2

# Neolithic / Agricultural Revolution

This week you will learn about the causes and consequences of the Agricultural Revolution, a time when people began to produce much of their food through farming.

**Directions:** Read the text below. Then answer the questions that follow.

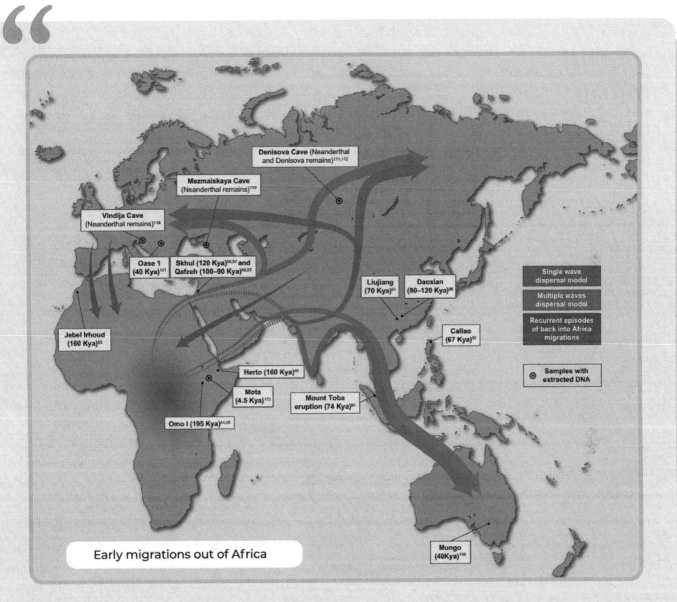

Early migrations out of Africa

For thousands of years, humans lived in small **nomadic** groups, traveling to different areas depending on the season and living off of wild plants and animals. **Archaeologists** (who study what these people left behind) refer to them as **hunter-gatherers**. Using weapons and tools made out of stone, these early humans hunted animals for meat and other supplies. They also gathered foods such as roots, nuts, and berries. These hunter-gatherers **migrated** from eastern Africa to areas all over the world. This time period is called the **Paleolithic era**, or the "old stone age."

About 10,000 years ago, a new pattern developed. Over time, hunter-gatherer groups began to settle into specific areas where they could stay all year. Instead of

> moving around to follow their food sources, they began to plant crops that could be harvested every year. This was the beginning of agriculture. This transition from nomadic hunter-gatherers to settled farming is the beginning of the Neolithic era. The **Neolithic era** means "new stone age" and is the beginning of the rest of human history up to today. Agriculture led to many major changes in how humans lived. As a result, this era is also called the Agricultural or Neolithic Revolution, and you will see both of those terms used in this book.

**1.** What does the term "Paleolithic" mean?

    **A.** New Stone Age     **C.** Old Stone Age

    **B.** Iron Age     **D.** Bronze Age

**2.** The transition to settled agriculture is known as

    **A.** The Industrial Revolution     **C.** The Green Revolution

    **B.** The Agricultural Revolution     **D.** The Technological Revolution

**3.** Which of the following things do archaeologists use to study ancient peoples?

    **A.** Tools

    **B.** Rock paintings

    **C.** Bones

    **D.** Pottery

    **E.** All of the above

**Directions:** Read the text below. Then answer the questions that follow.

Do you have any **domesticated** animals in your home? If you have a dog or a cat, you do! Domestication means that a species of plant or animal has been changed over time to benefit humans in some way. These changes make it easier to take care of the plants or animals, but it also means that they lose some of the skills they need to survive in the wild.

The Agricultural Revolution is characterized by the domestication of plants and animals. Sheep, goats, camels, cattle (cows), and pigs were some of the earliest domesticated animals. Animals can provide foods like meat and milk, as well as other products like furs and skins for leather. Some animals can also be used as **beasts of burden**, such as oxen for pulling wagons or heavy farming tools. Dogs were domesticated during this time as well, and were primarily used as guards for the animals as well as for companionship.

The domestication of plants takes a long time. Early farmers would find plants with the characteristics that they wanted (such as large edible fruit or seeds) and breed the plants to improve those characteristics year after year. Eventually, farmers developed reliable crops such as rice, oats, and wheat. They could be planted and harvested each year for a long-term food solution.

**Activity: Domesticating plants**

The process to domesticate plants takes many, many years. The domestication of corn is a great example of this process. Thousands of years ago, an ear of corn was known as teosinte. Teosinte was a cluster of tiny grains at the top of a stalk. An ancient farmer found a bunch of teosinte that looked different: the grains were larger and able to be removed, cooked, and eaten. This early farmer took some of the different grains and planted them. The next year, there were more edible grains. Each year, the farmers planted the best examples of the grain they wanted to harvest. Over time, they developed what we know today as maize or corn!

In the box below, draw each step of the process our farmer took from finding teosinte to eating a fresh ear of corn!

The Agricultural/Neolithic Revolution led to many changes. The hunter-gatherer way of life that had been practiced for thousands of years was evolving. Historians and archaeologists still debate whether or not this revolution was ultimately a good thing or a bad thing! You can see some of the arguments in the tables below.

### Settled Agriculture is Awesome!

| | |
|---|---|
| **1.** | More food is a good thing! With a more reliable food source, communities were able to feed a larger population. More food equals more people! |
| **2.** | In addition, with more people there are more workers. Eventually, **specialization of labor** developed. This meant that since the farmers were growing enough food for everyone, other people were able to focus, or specialize, in other important tasks. |
| **3.** | Because people were no longer traveling all year, they could build permanent houses, markets, and community buildings. They could also fill those buildings with stronger furniture, carpets, and evidence of their wealth. |
| **4.** | Large populations need someone in charge. New **government structures** were developed. |
| **5.** | Governments collect **taxes**! Someone needs to record that information. **Writing & record-keeping systems** were developed as a result of settled agriculture! |

**Directions:** Write 2-5 words that summarize each argument above.

Example: 1. More food = more people

1. .........................................................................................................................................

2. .........................................................................................................................................

3. .........................................................................................................................................

4. .........................................................................................................................................

## Settled Agriculture Causes Problems!

**1.** The domestication of animals led people and animals living close to each other. Many **diseases** developed that transferred back and forth between animals and humans. And since more people were living closer together, diseases spread between people as well.

**2.** Farmers often focused on just a few crops. Over time, people became less healthy because they weren't eating a variety of foods in their diet.

**3.** Plants were also at risk of disease. And if a disease wiped out the crop for the year, it could cause food scarcity. If they didn't have enough food for multiple years, it was considered a **famine**.

**4.** Many hunter-gatherer societies divided power between men and women in a more equal way. In larger agricultural societies, men were often given more power within families and in government. **Patriarchy**, a system where men hold most of the power, developed in most parts of the world.

**5.** Certain jobs and certain people had more importance in agricultural societies. This led to the development of **social classes**, where communities were led by a small group of wealthy, powerful people. Those with less wealth, or less-desirable jobs, did not have as much (or any) input into important decisions.

**Directions:** Write 2-5 words that summarize each argument above.

**1.** ....................................................................................................................

**2.** ....................................................................................................................

**3.** ....................................................................................................................

**4.** ....................................................................................................................

**5.** ....................................................................................................................

Yesterday you learned that one of the effects of the Neolithic Revolution was the development of **social classes**. The term "social" refers to **society**, or the organization, values, behaviors, etc. of people within a community. Society is one part of culture, and can be studied to learn how people within a group relate to each other. The diagram below is an example of a general social class structure that can be found throughout history.

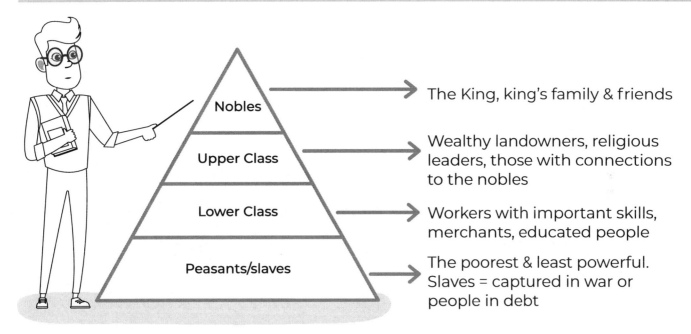

| Nobles | → The King, king's family & friends |
| Upper Class | → Wealthy landowners, religious leaders, those with connections to the nobles |
| Lower Class | → Workers with important skills, merchants, educated people |
| Peasants/slaves | → The poorest & least powerful. Slaves = captured in war or people in debt |

**Directions:** Draw a line from the description of each fictional person to the social class they are likely part of using the characteristics from the diagram above.

| NOBLES | UPPER CLASS | LOWER CLASS | PEASANTS/SLAVES |
|--------|-------------|-------------|-----------------|
| The scribe has spent his life learning to read and write, hoping to work as a tax collector | Even though he was captured in war, he was freed after his owner's death | As the king's sister, she has more control over her money compared to other women | His most important job is to lead religious services provide offerings to keep the gods happy |

### Social Classes Today

There are many historical factors that influence social class in the United States today. Much of U.S. history involves struggle between groups who are in power and groups who demand more power.

One constant feature of social classes throughout history has to do with wealth. Generally, those with more wealth have more power than those without. While wealth can be inherited through family members, it can also be earned through jobs.

Use the internet to research job listings in your area. Interview friends and family to learn about different jobs and salaries (how much workers are paid). Find 10 different jobs and salaries, and organize them from highest-paying at the top to lowest-paying at the bottom.

| Job Title | Salary |
|---|---|
| 1. | |
| 2. | |
| 3. | |
| 4. | |
| 5. | |
| 6. | |
| 7. | |
| 8. | |
| 9. | |
| 10. | |

What patterns can you identify by looking at the jobs and salaries on your list?

......................................................................................................................................................

......................................................................................................................................................

**Directions:** Read the text below. Then answer the question that follows.

This week you have looked at the importance of the Agricultural/Neolithic Revolution in human history. Use your work from the previous lessons to complete the following writing prompt.

Your response should include a <u>topic sentence</u> where you state your claim, <u>three to five pieces</u> of <u>evidence</u> that support your claim, and a <u>concluding sentence</u> that wraps up your paragraph.

The Agricultural Revolution had both positive and negative effects. Overall, do you feel that the positive effects outweigh the negative? Why or why not?

.........................................................................................................................................
.........................................................................................................................................
.........................................................................................................................................
.........................................................................................................................................
.........................................................................................................................................
.........................................................................................................................................
.........................................................................................................................................
..........................................................................................
..........................................................................................
..........................................................................................
..........................................................................................
..........................................................................................
..........................................................................................
..........................................................................................
..........................................................................................
..........................................................................................
..........................................................................................

# WEEK 3

# Mesopotamia & Egypt

This week you will learn about the Mesopotamians and Egyptians and their contributions to the ancient world.

ARGOPREP

**Directions:** Read the text below. Then answer the questions that follow.

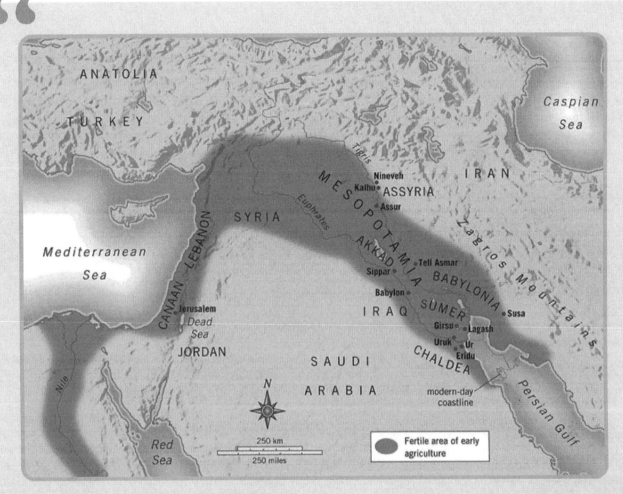

One of the earliest river settlements that developed into a **civilization** was along the banks of the Tigris and Euphrates Rivers. A civilization is a large, settled group that has characteristics that will come to represent population clusters around the world, such as cities with government buildings, education centers, and a wide variety of different types of jobs. Historians and archaeologists consider the Tigris and Euphrates river valleys to be part of the **Fertile Crescent**, an arc-shaped region with Mesopotamia in the east and the coast of the Mediterranean Sea in the west. The Tigris and Euphrates Rivers often flooded, which provided the region with fertile soil for agriculture. Unfortunately, this flooding was irregular and unpredictable. This frequently led to a loss of crops.

Another major civilization developed around the same time. All along the banks of the Nile River, in present-day Egypt, the predictable flooding of the Nile allowed people to safely plant and harvest their crops. The source of the Nile River is in Sub-Saharan Africa, and it flows north for thousands of miles before emptying into the

"

Mediterranean Sea. Convenient winds pushed boats upriver to settlements in the south, while the river currents carried them north towards settlements located along the banks.

Mesopotamia and Egypt both had primarily flat terrain or gently rolling hills, and **arid** desert climates. Rainfall was not very common. The soil was fertile due to the regular river flooding, but both civilizations developed **irrigation systems** as a way to transport water from the river to farmlands farther away. These irrigation systems allowed for even more food production and supported their growing populations. In addition, they both had **navigable** rivers, allowing for frequent trade and communication throughout each civilization.

"

1. What do you think the term **fertile** means?

   **A.** Excessive water

   **B.** Soil that is good for growing crops

   **C.** A region with frequent droughts

   **D.** Rivers that could be navigated

2. An "arid" climate is best described as

   **A.** Dry, not a lot of rainfall

   **B.** Frequent storms

   **C.** Lush and green

   **D.** An area with frequent earthquakes

3. Which of the following statements is true?

   **A.** Farmers in both regions developed irrigation systems that increased the available supply of food.

   **B.** Mesopotamian rivers flowed slowly, while the Nile River moved quickly and was difficult to navigate.

   **C.** Both regions were characterized by mild climates with seasonal rainfall.

   **D.** Since the populations were larger, the governments in both regions were based on representation.

**Directions:** Read the text below. Then answer the questions that follow.

If you've ever worked on a project with a group of people, you'll recognize the importance of having organization and leadership. The project will be most successful if everyone knows their role and there is a respected leadership structure. The same is true for large groups of people living together. As cities grew and civilizations flourished, government structures developed.

Both Mesopotamia and Egypt developed an **autocracy**. An autocracy is a government where one person has absolute power. In Mesopotamia, each city acted like its own country, and historians refer to them as city-states. Each **city-state** had its own king who was the final word on all decisions. Egypt was under the rule of the **pharaoh**. The pharaoh was an absolute ruler who was treated like a god and was both a religious and government leader. In both regions, the king or pharaoh had a variety of advisors and assistants that made sure that things were running smoothly.

In order for cities to be successful, there are many things that need to be built. Roads are a great example of something that is built and maintained by a government, but used by everyone. In order to maintain roads and other public structures, a government collects **taxes** from its citizens. Taxes could be in the form of money, food or other resources, or in the form of **labor** from people doing work for the government. In order to make sure that people were paying their taxes, a system of record-keeping needed to be developed. The Mesopotamian system of record-keeping is known as **cuneiform**, and was a series of symbols pressed into wet clay by a wedge-shaped stick called a **stylus**. A trained **scribe** would read and write these images and translate them for the recipient of the message.

The Egyptians developed a different system known as **hieroglyphics**. These were words and ideas represented by symbols and pictures. Egyptian scribes painted hieroglyphics on **papyrus**, which was an early form of paper. Papyrus was made by pressing and drying the stems of the papyrus plant that grew along the banks of the Nile. Hieroglyphics were also painted onto walls to record important events and stories.

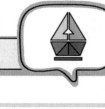
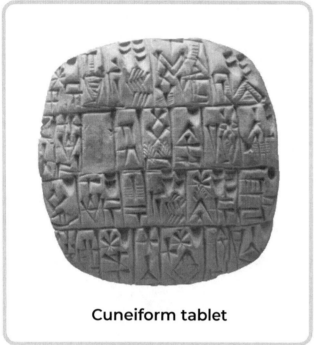

**Cuneiform tablet**

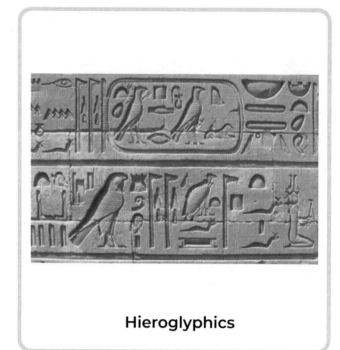

**Hieroglyphics**

1. What was writing used for?
   A. Record keeping
   B. Taxation
   C. Communication
   D. All of the above

2. What did Mesopotamians use for record keeping?
   A. Papyrus
   B. Paper
   C. Stylus and clay
   D. Wall paintings

3. What is papyrus made from?
   A. Paper
   B. A plant
   C. Silk
   D. Clay

**Directions:** Read the text below. Then answer the questions that follow.

The ancient river civilizations were greatly affected by the forces of nature. On Day 1 you learned that both Egypt and Mesopotamia were arid, desert climates with limited rainfall, and relied upon rivers for irrigation and fertile soil. But what if a flood washed away an entire harvest, or insects came through and ate the entire crop? How did people deal with catastrophic events like famine and warfare, as well as the issues of life and death that we still deal with today?

Mesopotamia and Egypt developed complex religious beliefs that were rooted in the power of nature. Gods were associated with different major forces, such as wind, sun, and water. They also had gods for pregnancy and childbirth, death, and the afterlife. A religion is considered **polytheistic** when it has multiple gods. (You will learn about **monotheistic** religions, or those with only one god, in a later chapter.) Each god had multiple roles, and people attempted to influence, or **appease** the gods by offering prayers and sacrifices.

It is interesting to compare the religious beliefs that developed in Egypt and Mesopotamia. Although they both had nature-based systems, their beliefs regarding life, death, and the afterlife were very different. Life in Mesopotamia was frequently characterized by unpredictable forces. The Tigris and Euphrates rivers would flood without warning. The flat terrain and city-state structure led to frequent warfare as kings attempted to gain more territory. Mesopotamian **mythology**, or stories about the gods, described the gods as selfish, chaotic and unpredictable, and the gods enjoyed toying with humans for their own entertainment. These stories helped Mesopotamians make sense of the tragedies that surrounded them. Interesting fact: We have many examples of Mesopotamian writing and stories, even though they lived thousands of years ago. How? Fire is a frequent companion to war. When clay is heated up, or "fired," it turns into durable pottery. As a result, the frequent warfare in Mesopotamia actually led to the preservation of Mesopotamian writing, because the clay tablets were preserved by the fires of war!

In contrast, Egyptian life was characterized by a series of **cycles**. Every day the sun rose and set. The Nile River flooded on a predictable schedule. The Nile River region was bordered by the Sahara Desert to the west, Mediterranean Sea to the north, the Red Sea to the east, and mountains to the south. Unlike the constant threat of warfare in Mesopotamia, thousands of years of Egyptian history are only rarely broken up by invasions. Therefore, Egyptian religious beliefs also revolved around cycles. Egyptians believed that the afterlife was a continuation of this life, and wealthy Egyptians would spend decades preparing their tombs with the items they would need in the afterlife.

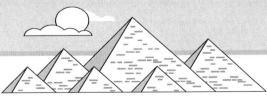

**Mesopotamian (Assyrian) bodies in a river, chaos & war**

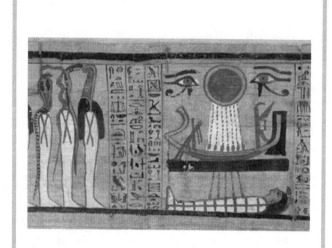

**Egyptian, moving into the afterlife**

**1.** How did ancient civilizations attempt to influence the actions of their gods?

..................................................................................................................

..................................................................................................................

**2.** Why did Mesopotamians believe that their gods were selfish, chaotic, and unpredictable?

..................................................................................................................

..................................................................................................................

**3.** What proof did Egyptians have that reinforced their belief in an afterlife?

..................................................................................................................

..................................................................................................................

**4.** Floods play a major role in Mesopotamian mythology. Why do you think this is?

..................................................................................................................

..................................................................................................................

..................................................................................................................

**Directions:** Read the text below. Then answer the questions that follow.

### The Code of Hammurabi

"If any one steal the property of a temple or of the court, he shall be put to death, and also the one who receives the stolen thing from him shall be put to death."

"If any one be too lazy to keep his dam in proper condition, and does not so keep it; if then the dam break and all the fields be flooded, then shall he in whose dam the break occurred be sold for money, and the money shall replace the corn which he has caused to be ruined."

"If a man put out the eye of another man, his eye shall be put out."

No matter how well you get along with the people around you, eventually there will be a disagreement. One of the things that civilizations need is a set of rules that all people have to follow. And in order for everyone to know the laws, it is important that they are written and shared. The Mesopotamians were the first to organize their laws into a clear system.

The Mesopotamian king Hammurabi had these laws carved into **stelae**, or stone pillars, and placed all around the kingdom. This way, everyone would know how to behave. The Code of Hammurabi was based on the concept of **retribution**, or the idea that the punishment should be equal to the crime. The idea is that people will avoid doing bad things because they know it would come back to hurt them. You may have heard the phrase "an eye for an eye." This phrase comes from the Code of Hammurabi and literally means that if you poke out someone's eye, your eye will then be poked out!

In addition to equal retribution, there were also different consequences based on social class. If a person of a higher class hurt someone lower than them, the penalty was much less severe. But if a lower-class person hurt someone of a higher class, the consequence would be much worse.

The modern criminal justice system has its roots in the laws of Mesopotamia, but we have different consequences for when laws are broken. Many people

> today disagree with justice based on retribution, and encourage **restorative justice**.
>
> Restorative justice seeks to examine the harmful impact of a crime and then determines what can be done to repair that harm while holding the person who caused it accountable for his or her actions...Rather than focusing on the punishment...restorative justice measures results by how successfully the harm is repaired.

Scenario: You are in the backyard practicing your baseball swing with wiffle balls. But you realize that hitting rocks is much more satisfying! Oh no! Your rock sails through the air and breaks the neighbor's window!

Retributive Justice: You are grounded, and your parents have to pay for the window. You have to do extra chores to pay them back.

Restorative Justice: You and your parents sit down with the neighbor and talk about your decision to hit rocks instead of wiffle balls. You realize that you weren't thinking about possible consequences, you were just having fun. This makes you realize that you have to think about your actions before you act on your ideas, and you acknowledge that your actions hurt your neighbor. Your parents agree to pay for the window, and you will learn a new skill by helping the neighbor install it.

Think of a scenario where a law has been broken or a crime has been committed. Describe what the consequence might look like from the perspective of retributive justice and restorative justice.

Scenario: ...................................................................................................................................

.............................................................................................................................................

Retributive Justice consequence: ....................................................................................

.............................................................................................................................................

Restorative Justice consequence: ...................................................................................

.............................................................................................................................................

.............................................................................................................................................

**Directions:** Read the text below. Then answer the questions that follow.

Did you know that many things you use every day were invented thousands of years ago? The ancient civilizations of Mesopotamia and Egypt came up with some pretty amazing ideas that we still use today!

The Mesopotamians invented the concept of dividing time into hours, minutes, and seconds. They created sundials and water clocks to keep track of time during the day and night.

The ancient Egyptians took timekeeping further by developing a calendar with 365 days, divided into 12 months. This calendar is very similar to the one we use today! One of the most important inventions in history came from Mesopotamia: the wheel! Around 3500 BCE, someone had the brilliant idea to use round objects to move heavy things more easily. This led to the creation of carts and chariots, making transportation much faster and easier.

Both Mesopotamians and Egyptians were skilled in **metallurgy** - the art of working with metals. They discovered how to extract metals from ore and create alloys like bronze. This knowledge allowed them to make stronger tools, weapons, and beautiful jewelry.

Believe it or not, the ancient Egyptians cared about dental hygiene too! They created a kind of toothpaste using ingredients like crushed rock salt, mint, dried iris flower, and pepper. While it might not taste as good as your minty fresh toothpaste, it helped keep their teeth clean.

These ancient inventions show us how clever and resourceful people were thousands of years ago. The next time you check the time, brush your teeth, or ride in a car, remember to thank the ancient Mesopotamians and Egyptians for their amazing ideas!

**Wheel**

**Iron**

**Mesopotamian sundial clock**

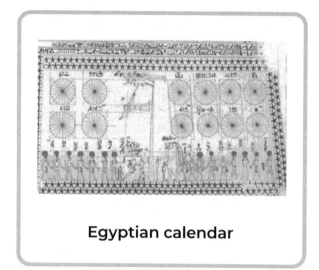

**Egyptian calendar**

One of the great things about new ideas is that they can be combined with other ideas to create something brand new! In the boxes below, think about how each of the inventions could be expanded upon to make something new. You can use ideas that already exist, or feel free to make up something new! Who knows, you might come up with a brand-new idea!

Example: Never-Late Alarm Clock: An alarm clock that wakes you up earlier if there's bad traffic or weather on your way to school.

| Ancient Invention | Modern Possibilities |
|---|---|
| **Clock** | |
| **Calendar** | |
| **Wheel** | |
| **Metallurgy** | |

# WEEK 4

# Indus River Valley

This week you will learn about the mysterious Indus River Valley civilization and the origins of Indian culture.

ARGOPREP

**Directions:** Read the text below. Then answer the questions that follow.

"

The Indus River flows through present-day Pakistan from the foothills of the Himalayas to the Arabian Sea. 4000 years ago, the Indus River Valley civilization established at least two main capitals at Mohenjo-daro and Harappa and many smaller settlements. The region flourished for over a thousand years and had regular trade with Mesopotamia. But eventually, the Indus River Valley civilization vanished.

This region of Pakistan has a climate that is very hot in the summer and very cold in the winter. This region is also characterized by the yearly **monsoons**. In an area with monsoons, the wind blows in one direction for part of the year, and then quickly shifts direction for the other part. The term "monsoon" refers to that seasonal shift in direction. As a result, a few months of the year have a lot of rain, while the rest of the year stays mostly dry. Understanding the monsoon patterns is incredibly important for people who live in a monsoon climate.

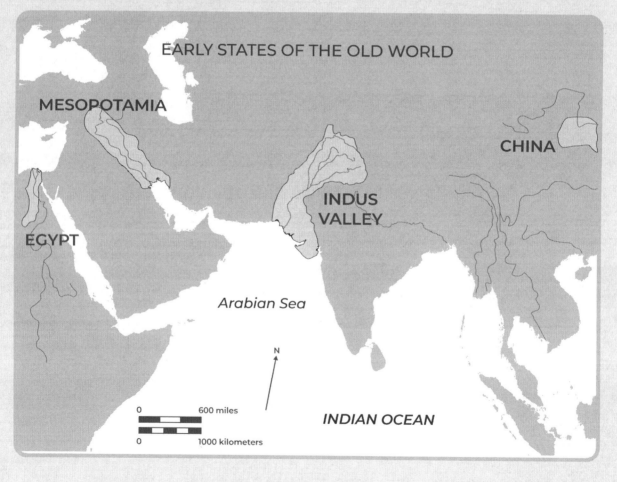

1. Using cardinal directions, where is the Indus River Valley in relation to Mesopotamia?
   A. Northeast
   B. Southeast
   C. Northwest
   D. Southwest

2. Using the scale at the bottom of the map, estimate how many miles are between the eastern part of the Indus River Valley region and the western part of Yellow River region of China.
   A. Approximately 2000 miles
   B. Approximately 1000 miles
   C. Exactly 300 miles
   D. Exactly 4000 miles

3. What is a "monsoon?"
   A. A dry, desert climate with infrequent rainfall
   B. A region with fertile soil and abundant rain
   C. The coldest period of the year when crops are dormant
   D. The shift in wind direction between the rainy season and the dry season

**Directions:** Read the text below. Then answer the questions that follow.

Many different people work together to piece together the stories of the past. We often think about the role of **historians** in studying history, but **anthropologists** and **archaeologists** are often the first ones to interact with the **artifacts** of the past. An artifact is something from a specific time period that can be studied. Artifacts can be as small as tiny bone fragments, or as large as massive tombs. Each artifact is examined by many different people who work together to determine a complete story about that object and the people who interacted with it.

**History**

Historians primarily rely on written records, either written by the people they are studying, or by people who interacted with them. Much of the written information we have about the Indus River Valley civilization is based on texts that were written by other people - people who traded with them or interacted with them in some way. We don't know a lot about what the Indus River Valley thought because we have not been able to translate their writing!

Archaeologists work with the physical objects that are left behind, like pottery, tools, and even bones! Archaeologists are experts at excavating and preserving ancient sites and artifacts. They are often responsible for literally putting the pieces together to tell a story of what has happened. Once the locations of Harappa and Mohenjo-daro were rediscovered, archaeologists worked to uncover the layers of the city that had been buried for centuries.

**Archaeology**

Anthropologists study how people interact with each other. Anthropologists use the artifacts uncovered by archaeologists to determine how people related to each other, what their culture was like, how they worshiped, etc. Modern anthropologists might study a specific group of people, such as an isolated Amazonian tribe, or the behaviors of American teenagers. As we learn more about the writing system of the Indus River Valley, anthropologists will be able to learn more about the people who lived there.

**Anthropology**

Scenario: A historian, an anthropologist, and an archaeologist all visit a museum. Describe three things that each person would spend their time studying while they are there!

Historian: ...........................................................................................................................................................
................................................................................................................................................................................
................................................................................................................................................................................
................................................................................................................................................................................

Archaeologist: ...................................................................................................................................................
................................................................................................................................................................................
................................................................................................................................................................................

Anthropologist: .................................................................................................................................................
................................................................................................................................................................................
................................................................................................................................................................................
................................................................................................................................................................................

**Directions:** Read the text below. Then answer the questions that follow.

"

   In Week 3 you learned about the importance of clear leadership and government structure in making sure a civilization runs smoothly. Unfortunately, much of the written language of the Indus River Valley has not yet been deciphered. We must rely on archaeological findings and evidence from other civilizations to learn about the people who lived here. While we don't know much about the governments of Harappa and Mohenjo-daro, we can make some assumptions. Based on what has been found, historians believe that Harappa and Mohenjo-daro must have been part of a larger government system because they had a remarkable number of similarities.

   Even though the cities were approximately 400 miles apart (that's about the distance from New York City to Maine or North Carolina), they were organized in similar ways. The most obvious one is the layout of streets and blocks. Both cities had what urban geographers call a "grid system." That means that the majority of the streets criss-cross the city and intersect at 90-degree angles. Most ancient cities grew as the population grew, and streets were added as needed (many ancient city maps look like a plate of spaghetti!) The grid system is evidence that the cities were planned out ahead of time, the earliest known example of "urban planning."

   One of the most fascinating things about Harappa and Mohenjo-daro is that they had indoor plumbing! Each house had access to a well, and had separate spaces for bathing and toilet use. Water was drawn up from the well and used, and then poured down a drain. The drain was connected to the other houses on the block and angled so that the wastewater from each house would be flushed out to a main wastewater tank that was located outside of the city. In addition to a centralized plumbing system, these cities also had garbage service that would travel house to house and collect trash on a regular basis. These two things sound normal for people living in cities today, but this was incredibly rare in the ancient world!

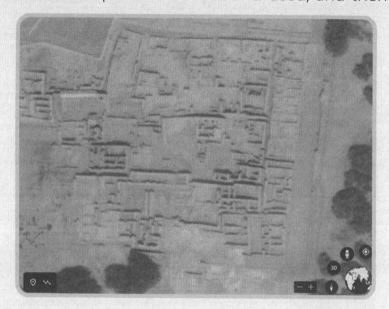

**1.** The two major cities of the Indus River Valley civilization, Harappa and Mohenjo-daro, are believed to have been part of a larger government structure. What evidence from the text supports this idea?

............................................................................................................................

............................................................................................................................

............................................................................................................................

**2.** On Day 2 you learned about the different tools and methods that are used by historians, archaeologists, and anthropologists. Describe how a person from each of these disciplines would go about studying the Indus River Valley civilization.

Historians: ....................................................................................................

............................................................................................................................

............................................................................................................................

Archaeologists: ...........................................................................................

............................................................................................................................

............................................................................................................................

Anthropologists: .........................................................................................

............................................................................................................................

............................................................................................................................

**Directions:** Read the text below. Then follow the instructions to complete the activity.

> The term "culture" is frequently used when studying groups of people. But sometimes culture can be very difficult to explain. Everything that an individual person does or believes is part of their culture. Each person is unique. But culture is also something that a group of people share. Civilizations are made up of individuals, but when certain characteristics are frequently found, then those become elements of that group's culture.

We are still learning about the Indus River Valley culture. Until we are able to decipher all of their writings we will continue to theorize about who they were. But based on the things we do know, we can develop some theories about Harappan culture.

| Observation | Theory |
|---|---|
| From the excavations of buildings in Mohenjo-daro, archaeologists have been unable to find evidence of wealthy homes. | It seems that there was not a major difference within social classes. |
| There is no evidence of an army or other characteristics of warfare | The Indus River Valley may have been a peaceful settlement with very little conflict |
| Very precise weights and measurements have been found | Math, science, and other subjects were probably taught. Trade was very important |
| Each house had access to clean water and sanitation | Not only was cleanliness important, but the government took responsibility for maintaining the cities |

Scenario: It is 2000 years in the future. The world has become a very different place. A future archaeologist has found your house and is currently studying the contents. Identify five things they may find, and describe what theories they may come up with to better understand Earth of the early 21st century.

| Observation/Object | Theory |
|---|---|
|  |  |
|  |  |
|  |  |
|  |  |
|  |  |

**Directions:** Read the text below. Then follow the instructions to complete the activity.

"

After nearly two thousand years of development, the Indus River Valley civilization disappears from history. We have not been able to decipher most of the writings that we have, so historians do not have a lot of evidence to work with. Some people believe that some of the Harappan culture was absorbed into later groups who moved into the region, while other historians argue that there is very little evidence to support that theory.

One thing that most people can agree on, however, is that something drastic happened which caused the Indus River Valley populations to move. Settlements with similar characteristics to Harappa and Mohenjo-daro have been found further upriver in the foothills of the Himalayas. Climate historians claim that a decrease in reliable rain during the monsoon seasons could have pushed the Harappans into the hills. Other theories are that the Indus River could have changed course, isolating the cities that relied on it. While it seems extreme, it is not uncommon for a river to change course. Major flooding or an earthquake could cause a shift in the path of the river, swamping one area while leaving the docks of another area high and dry.

**Harappan boat found at Mohenjo-daro**

Scientists who study climate change look at geological records to learn about what has happened in the past. They can look at long-term patterns, such as what happens over a thousand years, by analyzing different parts of a river or stream. Today, scientists and historians are still trying to determine what happened to the people of the Indus River Valley, and perhaps make predictions for the future.

"

Climate change is affecting our planet in many ways. Some places might see more rain and flooding, while others might have hotter summers or colder winters. Let's find out what might happen in your area! Ask your parents, teachers, or local librarian to help you find information about climate change in your area. You can also research online to find information specific to your area. Describe what you have learned below!

# WEEK 5

# Yellow River, China

This week you will learn about ancient China and the foundations of Chinese culture.

ARGOPREP

**Directions:** Read the text below. Then answer the questions that follow.

The Yellow River (or Huang He) flows from the highlands in western China all the way to the Yellow Sea and the Pacific Ocean. The Yellow River gets its name from the yellow **silt** (tiny pieces of soil) that it carries along the way. When the river floods, this silt settles into the farmlands along its bank and provides fertile soil for crops. The Yangtze River is to the south and also provides fertile soil. Many civilizations developed along these river valleys.

The climate in this region is also characterized by the yearly **monsoons**. Much like the Indus River Valley, it is important to know the monsoon patterns so that valuable crops are not planted at the wrong time. Heavy rains can wipe out an entire crop!

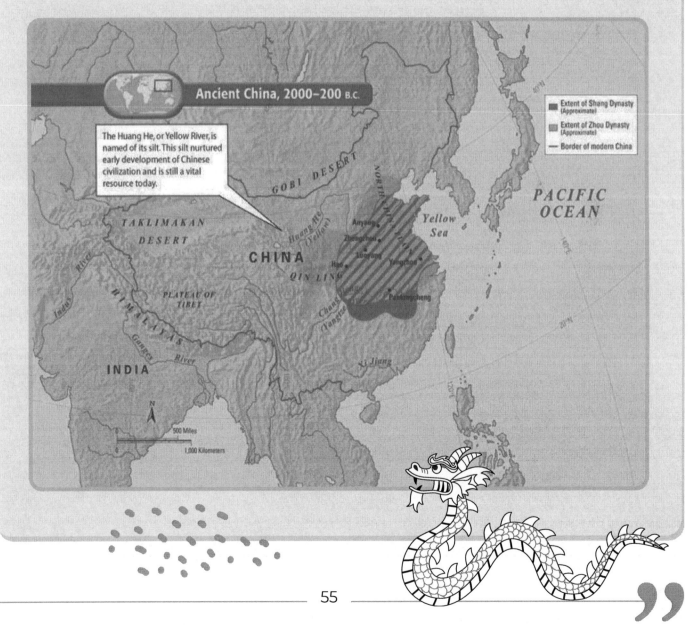

# Week 5
## Day 1

**Geography & Climate**

ENGAGING WITH THE TOPIC

**1.** Why is silt good for farming?
   **A.** It provides a barrier to keep the river from flooding
   **B.** It makes the river flow faster
   **C.** It provides the soil with important nutrients
   **D.** It removes nutrients from the soil

**2.** Which river runs along the southern region of ancient China?
   **A.** Huang He (Yellow) River
   **B.** Yangtzee River
   **C.** Indus River
   **D.** Euphrates river

**3.** What geographic feature separates India from China?
   **A.** Taklamakan Desert
   **B.** Gobi Desert
   **C.** Yellow Sea
   **D.** Himalayas

**Directions:** Examine the diagram below. Then answer the questions that follow.

When studying history, you'll often encounter dates followed by the letters BCE or CE. These letters are crucial for understanding when events occurred in the past. BCE stands for "Before Common Era," while CE stands for "Common Era." You might also be familiar with the terms BC (Before Christ) and AD (Anno Domini, Latin for "in the year of our Lord"), which are used in the same way.

This dating system is centered around a specific point in time: the traditionally believed year of Jesus Christ's birth, which is designated as year zero. All years counted backwards from this point are labeled BCE or BC, while all years counted forward are labeled CE or AD.

You can think of this system like a number line, with zero at the center. Years to the left of zero are BCE, counting backwards, while years to the right are CE, counting forwards. For example, the pyramids of Egypt were built around 2560 BCE, which would be far to the left on our imaginary timeline. On the other hand, the United States declared independence in 1776 CE, placing it to the right of our center point.

It's important to understand that even though this system originated from Christian history, it's widely used by historians to organize historical events from all cultures and religions. Many cultures have their own calendar systems, but the BCE/CE (or BC/AD) system provides a common reference point for discussing history on a global scale.

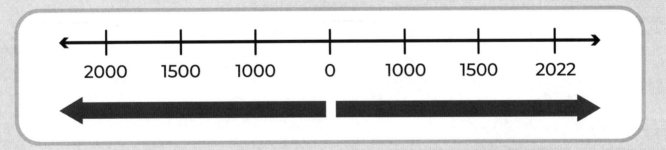

2000   1500   1000   0   1000   1500   2022

### Chinese Dynasties

| | |
|---|---|
| ca. 2100 - 1600 BCE | Xia Dynasty |
| ca. 1600 - 1050 BCE | Shang Dynasty |
| 1046 - 256 BCE | Zhou Dynasty |
| 221 - 206 BCE | Qin Dynasty |
| 206 BCE - 220 CE | Han Dynasty |
| 220 - 589 CE | Six Dynasties Period |
| 581 - 618 CE | Sui Dynasty |
| 618 - 906 CE | Tang Dynasty |
| 907 - 960 CE | Five Period |
| 581 - 618 CE | Sui Dynasties |
| 618 - 906 CE | Tang Dynasty |
| 907-960 CE | Five Dynasties Period |
| 960 - 1279 CE | Song (Sung) Dynasty |

Chinese history is divided up into **dynasties**. A dynasty is when power is passed down through the same family group for dozens or even hundreds of years! Dynasties get their name either from the area where the leaders are from, or by the name of the person who gains the power to rule. When we talk about events in Chinese history, we use the name of the dynasty first, then the year (if necessary). You'll notice that the Han Dynasty begins in 206 BCE and ends in 220 CE. That means the Han Dynasty began 206 years before 0 and ended 220 years after 0. The Dynasties before the Han were all BCE, and those that come after are all labeled CE.

**1.** How long was the Han Dynasty?

    **A.** 426 years

    **B.** 212 years

    **C.** 268 years

    **D.** 945 years

**2.** Which is the oldest Chinese dynasty?

    **A.** Xia Dynasty

    **B.** Zhou Dynasty

    **C.** Qin Dynasty

    **D.** Ming Dynasty

**3.** The abbreviation "ca." stands for the Latin word *circa*, which means around, or approximately. Why do historians use "ca." instead of a specific year?

    **A.** They are not sure if the event really happened

    **B.** They are not sure if the event happened in B.C.E. or C.E.

    **C.** They know that the event happened, but not the exact year

    **D.** There is enough evidence to be confident about when the event happened

**Directions:** Read the text below. Then answer the questions that follow.

As you learned on Day 2, Chinese history is organized by dynasties. Each era is known by the dynasty that was ruling China at that time. Each dynasty is made up of multiple specific leaders, known as Emperors (and occasionally Empresses). But as you saw on the Day 2 timeline, there have been many dynasties throughout Chinese history. What would happen to cause a new dynasty to begin?

Let's start with the Chinese concept of "Heaven." To the ancient Chinese, Heaven was not a place. It was the concept of an ultimate power that ruled over everything. At times it is understood as a supreme god or **deity**. Other times it is described as the overall law of nature. Either way, if the leader is following the "way" of heaven (the **dao**) then good things would happen. A good harvest, a successful battle, or a productive flood season are all examples of how Heaven rewards an emperor who is ruling according to the dao. This favor, or **mandate**, shows that the emperor has the support of Heaven. This is called the **Mandate of Heaven**. And if Heaven supports the emperor, then the people will as well!

But an emperor can lose the Mandate of Heaven. If bad things start happening, like natural disasters, a poor harvest, or a series of invasion, that would be evidence that the emperor is no longer ruling according to the dao, and is losing the Mandate of Heaven. And if the emperor no longer has the support of Heaven, then the people will begin to rebel. The combination of natural disasters and civil unrest will cause the dynasty to collapse. Over time, a new family will build up support and rise to power. As things begin to stabilize, this family will claim the Mandate of Heaven. A new dynasty takes hold as society enters into an era of peace, stability, and growth. This process is known as the **dynastic cycle**, and is repeated throughout Chinese history.

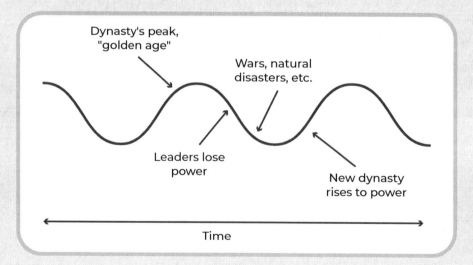

**1.** Which term best matches the concept of "mandate?"

   **A.** Approval

   **B.** Disagreement

   **C.** Opposite

   **D.** Disobedience

**2.** The "dao" can be best described by which of the following?

   **A.** The proper way to rule

   **B.** To live according to the expectations of Heaven

   **C.** To do the "right" things

   **D.** All of the above

**3.** Which of the following is evidence that the leader is losing the Mandate of Heaven?

   **A.** A flood arrives as expected and makes irrigation easier.

   **B.** An invasion from the north is successfully fought off.

   **C.** An earthquake causes the river to shift away from the city.

   **D.** A stretch of good weather leads to an abundant harvest.

"

Imagine a normal day. You didn't sleep well, and woke up cranky. You snap at your little brother who screams and throws his cereal across the room, hitting your dad as he walks into the kitchen. He gets annoyed because he has to go change, and you are all now late for school and work. You all leave the house feeling grumpy, and you spread that bad mood to others that you meet. This is an example of a morning where your family was not in **harmony** with each other. The concept of harmony is found in music when different notes are played together to create a more full and pleasant sound. In society, harmony is when everyone is working together to fulfill their duties, and it is what makes society run smoothly. Ancient Chinese beliefs revolve around the concept of a harmonious society.

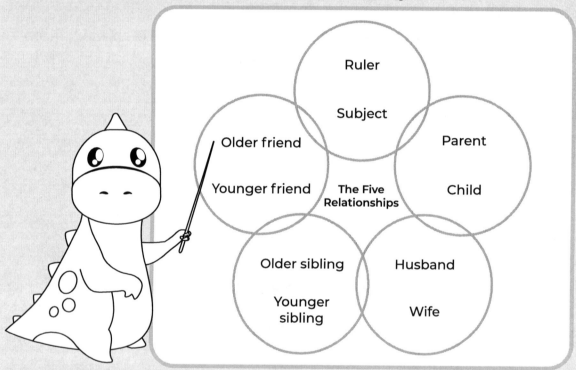

The Chinese philosopher **Confucius** lived during the Zhou Dynasty. His teachings, later called **Confucianism**, became the foundation for much of Chinese culture. At the heart of Confucianism is the idea that every person plays a role in society through the **Five Relationships**. For example, it is a parent's duty to care for a child. And it is the child's duty to be obedient to the parent. If both people fulfill their duty, their relationship will be harmonious. If everyone fulfills their duty in each of their relationships, then society will be harmonious. These relationships are often based on power and authority. The person with more power is responsible for the person with less. And the person with less power is taught to be obedient to those with more. In Confucianism, the balance within each of these relationships ultimately balances the society.

"

**Directions:** Read the text below. Then answer the questions that follow.

Think about how you have been taught to interact with others. Can you find examples of a "more power - less power" relationship (for example, teacher and student). Write down a few examples of this type of relationship. Then, describe how that relationship works within society as a whole. Does it help maintain harmony? Or does it cause things to be unbalanced? Do you think this system is a good way for large numbers of people to coexist?

" Used by nearly a quarter of the population today, the Chinese writing system goes back thousands of years. Similar to the Egyptians, the Chinese developed pictographs that represented specific objects or ideas. These symbols are known as characters. Variations of these **characters** can also be found in written Japanese and Korean.

The earliest examples of Chinese characters are found on **oracle bones** and were used as a way to communicate with the gods. Questions were written on various animal bones, which were then heated until cracks formed. Religious leaders would interpret the location of the cracks and translate their meanings. Over time, the characters evolved into the versions that are studied today. It is actually possible for many people who are fluent in written Chinese to read things that were written over a thousand years ago!

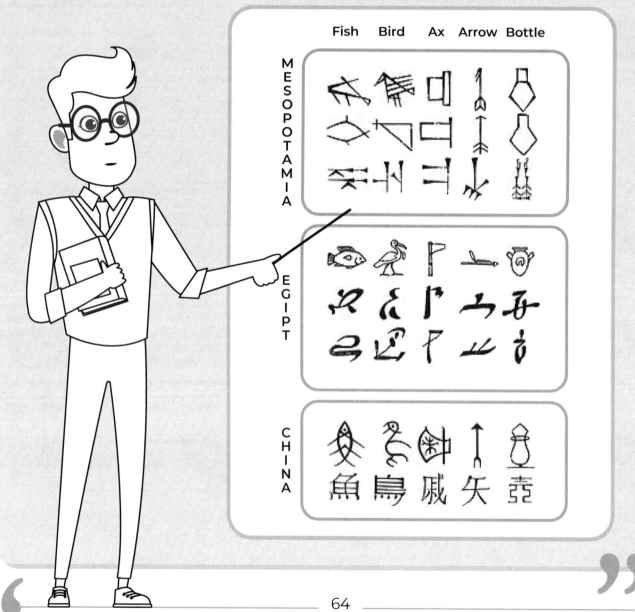

One of the most recent changes to written languages around the world has been the result of text messaging! From "text speak" to emojis, language continues to evolve. In the boxes below, write five ideas that you often use in text or instant messaging. For each idea, write the "text speak" version, and then draw the emoji version that you use with your friends or family.

| Idea | Text version | Emoji |
|---|---|---|
| Example: Laughter, sharing that something is funny | LOL (laugh out loud) | |
| | | |
| | | |
| | | |
| | | |
| | | |

# WEEK 6

# Religions of East and South Asia

Hinduism

Buddhism

This week you will learn about the religious beliefs that developed in East and South Asia, and how they spread and influenced the surrounding areas.

ARGOPREP

**Directions:** Read the text below. Then answer the questions that follow.

Over the past few weeks we have learned about the ancient societies of the Eastern Hemisphere. The next few weeks will focus on the belief systems that developed in each region. Some of these systems involve the belief and worship of a **deity** (a god or divine being), and are called **religions**. Religions often have a specific location or person that is honored. In some religions that person is worshiped like a deity. In others that person is not a deity, but is honored and respected as an important leader or founder. In addition to acts of worship, religions also set rules and expectations for behavior, such as wearing certain clothes or not eating certain foods. Most religions also have beliefs regarding what happens after we die.

Other belief systems are more focused on how to live a fulfilling life. These don't involve worship of a deity, and are referred to as **philosophies**. A philosophy is more focused on day-to-day actions as opposed to what happens after death. In some cultures, a philosophy can exist along with a religion. Rules and expectations for behavior can also be part of a philosophy.

The religions and philosophies of Confucianism, Hinduism, Buddhism, (and later, Sikhism) all developed alongside the cultures of the East and South Asian regions.

Last week you learned about some of the basic teachings of the Chinese philosopher Kong-fu-zi (or Confucius, as European cultures would later call him). He collected and documented beliefs that had already existed for centuries. Confucianism is the collection of those teachings as taught by Confucius. The importance of knowing and fulfilling one's duty in the family and society is the core idea of Confucianism and has influenced not only Chinese culture, but also the societies of Korea and Japan. For some, Confucianism is considered a religion due to the importance of honoring and communicating with ancestors. For others, however, Confucianism does not have a deity, so it is more of a philosophy that can exist with other religious beliefs. Many people in present-day China do not believe in a specific religion, however they practice Confucianism in many aspects of their culture.

After the mysterious collapse of the Indus River Valley civilization, Indian history shifts to the northern and eastern parts of India. The beliefs that make up **Hinduism** originated during this period. Hindus believe in the concept of **karma**. Karma is the energy generated by a person's actions. If someone does good things, they generate good karma. Bad things generate bad karma. Hindus also believe in **reincarnation**. Reincarnation is the belief that when a person dies, their soul is reborn into another body. The karma of a person's past lives determines the social class they are born into in their next life. Good karma will reincarnate someone into a higher class than bad karma. For Hindus, it is important to do good deeds in order to generate good karma

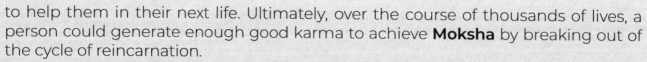

to help them in their next life. Ultimately, over the course of thousands of lives, a person could generate enough good karma to achieve **Moksha** by breaking out of the cycle of reincarnation.

Since Hinduism developed a long time ago, and has so many followers, different groups have developed their own distinct ways of worship - there is no one set of rules that are followed by all Hindus. In general, Hindus worship an ultimate god, **Brahma**. Brahma takes many forms and many names (such as Shiva and Vishnu), and each form is connected to different aspects of life. In Week 3 you learned about nature-based gods. Hindu deities take on similar characteristics. Some Hindus recognize the different forms of Brahma as individual deities. This is one example of how Hinduism is practiced in a variety of different ways.

**1.** Which of the following is true of a philosophy?

   **A.** A philosophy doesn't focus on the worship of a specific deity

   **B.** A philosophy doesn't provide rules and expectations for behavior.

   **C.** A society can have only one philosophical belief.

   **D.** A philosophy focuses primarily on what happens after death.

**2.** Which of the following is a major focus of Confucianism?

   **A.** What happens after death

   **B.** Following a specific set of daily activities

   **C.** Fulfilling one's duty to the family and society

   **D.** Participating in yearly celebrations

**3.** In Hinduism, which of the following determines a person's placement in the next life?

   **A.** Moksha       **B.** Karma       **C.** Nirvana       **D.** Shiva

**4.** Based on what you've learned so far, do you think Hinduism is a monotheistic or polytheistic religion? Explain your answer.

.................................................................................................................................................

.................................................................................................................................................

.................................................................................................................................................

**Directions:** Read the text below. Then answer the questions that follow.

Religious beliefs often shift over time. Each generation passes on the teachings of their ancestors, but they might also change how those beliefs are practiced. Today, we will explore some additional belief systems that developed in northern India: Buddhism and Sikhism.

During the 500s BCE, a young Hindu prince named Siddartha Gautama was moved to abandon his life of luxury after experiencing the suffering of life outside his palace walls. He came to understand that suffering is the result of attachment to the things of the world, and by living a life without being burdened by these attachments, one can reach ultimate **enlightenment** and break the cycle of reincarnation. Instead of being reincarnated, an enlightened soul reaches an ultimate state of peace known as **Nirvana**. While Hindus believe this takes thousands of lives, a Buddhist could potentially break the cycle of reincarnation and suffering by deeply following Buddhist teachings within one single life. Simple living and meditation are common practices of a Buddhist.

One who has reached enlightenment is known as a buddha. Siddartha Gautama was the first to reach enlightenment and is known as the Buddha, and his teachings known as Buddhism. Since it developed out of Hinduism, there are some similarities between Hindu and Buddhist beliefs, such as karma and reincarnation. Buddhism is primarily considered a philosophy, because the Buddha was a teacher, not a deity. Because of this, it is attractive to people from many different cultures and ultimately spread and took hold in regions outside of India. Buddhism is practiced alongside Confucianism in China, coexists with the Shinto beliefs of Japan, and also spread to Korea, Vietnam, and other areas of southeast Asia.

Confucianism, Hinduism, and Buddhism all developed prior to 500 BCE. Much later, in the 1400s CE, **Sikhism** also emerged from northern India. Sikhism is a monotheistic religion focusing on the teachings of Guru Nanak, the first **guru**, or teacher, of the Sikh religion. Nine more gurus spread the teachings of Guru Nanak until Guru Gobind Singh established the complete teachings of Sikhism in the late 1600s.

Sikhism teaches that there is one single God, and it is possible for every person to merge, or become one with God. To do this, one must focus on this goal through daily meditation, living an honest and truthful life, and by making it a priority to help others through good works and service. While there are many different groups of people practicing Sikhism, all of them work towards the goal of equality. To truly care for others, one must treat them as an equal. Sikhs work to limit inequalities related to social class and gender. While the majority of Sikhs are found in India, Sikh communities can be found in countries all over the world.

**1.** What is reincarnation?

    **A.** The Buddhist afterlife.

    **B.** When the soul achieves Nirvana

    **C.** The Sikh practice of covering their hair.

    **D.** When the soul is reborn into a new body.

**2.** Which of the following is a primary focus of Sikhism?

    **A.** Equality      **B.** Karma      **C.** Wealth      **D.** Conversion

**3.** Which of the following practices is shared by Buddhism and Sikhism?

    **A.** Nirvana      **B.** Meditation      **C.** Moksha      **D.** Baptism

**4.** Why can Buddhism exist alongside other religious beliefs?

..............................................................................................................................

..............................................................................................................................

..............................................................................................................................

**Directions:** Read the text in the table below. Then answer the questions that follow.

| Belief System | Hinduism | Buddhism | Sikhism | Confucianism |
|---|---|---|---|---|
| **Origin/ Founder/ Dates** | Origin unknown; collection of beliefs prior to 1000 BCE, India | Siddhartha Gautama, 500s BCE, India | Guru Nanak, 1400s CE, India | Kong-fu-zi (Confucius), 500s BCE, China |
| **Basic Beliefs** | **Reincarnation**: the soul is reborn into a different body after death. A person's current life is based on **karma**, or energy generated by their actions in a previous life. Multiple lifetimes of generating good karma (by doing good things, following the laws, etc.) will result in achieving **Moksha**, and breaking the cycle of reincarnation. | Life is characterized by suffering; the way to end suffering is to give up attachments and achieve **enlightenment**. Once a person has achieved enlightenment, they can break the cycle of suffering and reincarnation and achieve **Nirvana**. | Achieve one-ness with God by living according to the three core pillars: Daily meditation to keep the mind focused on God, earning a truthful and honest living, and caring for others through service, charity, and working towards equality. | Accepting and fulfilling one's duty within the family and society, and contributing to a harmonious existence with the world.<br><br>For some, Confucianism includes religious beliefs and activities. For others, it is part of daily life and exists alongside other religious beliefs. |
| **Current Global Distribution** | South Asia (India, Nepal) | East and Southeast Asia (China, Japan, Thailand, Myanmar, Bhutan, Cambodia) | India (Additional populations clusters in Australia, United States, Canada) | China (Confucian principles have also strongly influenced Japanese and Korean cultures) |
| **Importance of converting others** | Low. Anyone can choose to practice the teachings of Hinduism but Hindus do not actively seek converts. | Medium. Buddhists seek to teach others how to live a life without suffering | Low. Anyone can choose to practice the teachings of Sikhism but Sikhs do not actively seek converts. | Low. Primarily spread as a way of daily life in East Asian cultures as opposed to adoption of religious practices |

1. Which of the following present-day countries is the origin of multiple religions?
   **A.** China

   **B.** Japan

   **C.** India

   **D.** Pakistan

2. Of the four religions in the chart above, Buddhism has the most followers spread out over multiple countries. Why do you think Buddhism is found in so many places with different cultures?

..............................................................................................................

..............................................................................................................

..............................................................................................................

..............................................................................................................

..............................................................................................................

..............................................................................................................

**Directions:** Look at the map below. It shows where Buddhism started (origin) and how it spread throughout Asia.

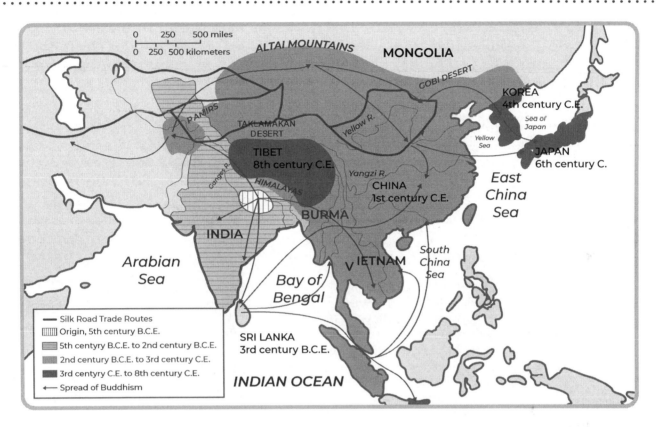

1. Where did Buddhism originate? ..............................................................................................

2. Name one place where Buddhism spread during the 3rd - 8th centuries CE.

...................................................................................................................................................................

3. According to the map, Tibet is closer to India than some of the other places where Buddhism spread. Why do you think Buddhism took so much longer to reach Tibet?

...................................................................................................................................................................
...................................................................................................................................................................
...................................................................................................................................................................
...................................................................................................................................................................
...................................................................................................................................................................
...................................................................................................................................................................

**Directions:** Read the text below. Follow the instructions to complete the activity.

Think back on when you were a young child. Perhaps you had a special stuffed animal or a blanket that you took everywhere. This item was incredibly important to you, and if it was ever lost or broken, you were likely inconsolable. This blanket or stuffed animal was almost **sacred** to you. The word "sacred" means that something holds incredible importance to someone. It usually refers to something that is connected to a religious belief, such as a sacred object or a sacred location. Places and objects that are sacred are usually connected to the religious founder or an important event. A religion can also have sacred texts and celebrations.

Your childhood object had incredible importance to you. But to someone else, it may have just looked like an old toy or ratty blanket with holes. They didn't understand its importance, and didn't care about it as much as you did. Things that are sacred in the religious beliefs of one person may be ignored or misunderstood by other people. It is important to recognize that just because a place or object isn't important to you, it can still have incredible importance to someone else.

The following chart shows a few examples of something that is sacred to each of the belief systems we have studied this week. It is important to treat people with respect, even if you may not understand their beliefs.

| Religion | Sacred Ideas/Places/Objects |
|---|---|
| **Hinduism** | Cows are considered sacred, and it is against the law to injure or kill a cow. Many Hindus are vegetarian due to a belief of nonviolence to all living things, including killing animals for food. |
| **Buddhism** | Temples are sacred spaces for Buddhists to meditate. The Buddha is not worshiped; statues within a temple are there to help people focus on their meditations. Temples may be at a sacred location (likely a place that the Buddha visited) or they may have a **relic**, or something that originally belonged to the Buddha. |
| **Sikhism** | Sikhs do not cut their hair out of respect for how they were created by God. Sikh men wear their long hair wrapped up in a distinctive turban and will often maintain full beards. |
| **Confucianism** | Honoring the ancestors (ancestor veneration) is a way to fulfill one's duty to their deceased family members. Many houses contain a family shrine where people leave offerings to those who have died. Some people believe that the spirits of their ancestors can influence what happens in the lives of the living. |

**1.** Which of these belief systems were you most familiar with? Least familiar? Write a paragraph that summarizes your experiences with people of different religious beliefs.

.................................................................................................................................

.................................................................................................................................

.................................................................................................................................

.................................................................................................................................

.................................................................................................................................

.................................................................................................................................

.................................................................................................................................

.................................................................................................................................

# WEEK 7

# Religions of Southwest Asia and Europe

This week you will learn about the religious beliefs that developed in Southwest Asia and Europe, and how they spread globally in later centuries.

ARGOPREP

**Directions:** Read the text below. Then answer the questions that follow.

This week we will return to Mesopotamia to start our study of religions that developed in Southwest Asia (also known as the Middle East), North Africa, and Europe. We will also be looking at a religion that developed in ancient Persia, or present-day Iran. These belief systems will be divided into two groups: The Abrahamic Religions (Judaism, Christianity, and Islam) and the Persian religion of Zoroastrianism.

You will recall from Week 3 that the various groups in Mesopotamia were polytheistic. Each city-state worshiped different deities, although they were all part of the same **pantheon**, or group of gods. One particular tribe known as the Israelites followed a monotheistic path, meaning they only acknowledged the existence of a single god. The leader of the Israelites was a man named Abraham. The religions of Judaism, Christianity, and Islam will all develop from Abraham's descendants.

Jews believe that Abraham made a **covenant**, or agreement with the god Yahweh. Abraham agreed that his tribe and their descendants will recognize Yahweh as the only God. In exchange, the Israelites would be God's chosen people and would be returned to the land of Israel. The Jewish community and the teachings of Judaism trace back to Abraham through his son Isaac. Jews show their faith through many day-to-day activities, such as only eating **kosher** food. Kosher means that the food was prepared according to Jewish law. Another important practice is Yom Kippur, when Jews reflect on the previous year and ask forgiveness for their sins.

Another religion that developed around the same time as Judaism was in Persia, in present-day Iran. The Persians practiced a religion known as Zoroastrianism. The beliefs of Zoroastrianism are based on the writings of the prophet Zarathustra (known as Zoroaster by people in Greece). Ahura Mazda is the main god and is represented by goodness and light. Ahura Mazda is in a constant struggle with an evil spirit known as Ahriman, who is represented by darkness and evil. To support Ahura Mazda, people must constantly choose positive actions, thoughts, and behavior. Zoroastrians use fire in their rituals as a representation of Ahura Mazda. Although Zoroastrians make up a tiny fraction of the population today, many historians and religious scholars believe that Judaism (and therefore Christianity and Islam) was heavily influenced by Zoroastrian beliefs.

**1.** Who was the founder of Judaism?

    **A.** Ahura Mazda      **B.** Jesus      **C.** Isaac      **D.** Abraham

**2.** The ancient empire of Persia was in which present-day country?

    **A.** Iran

    **B.** Iraq

    **C.** Israel

    **D.** Egypt

**3.** Why do Zoroastrians use fire in their worship practices?

    **A.** To represent Ahura Mazda

    **B.** To represent Ahriman

    **C.** To keep warm

    **D.** To prepare food for sacrifices

**4.** Which characteristic is shared by Judaism and Zoroastrianism?

    **A.** They both started in present-day Iraq

    **B.** They worship the same deity

    **C.** They are both monotheistic

    **D.** They both started in present-day Israel

**Directions:** Read the text below. Then answer the questions that follow.

> Around 1500 years after the development of Judaism, another group emerged in present-day Israel. For centuries, Jewish prophets spoke of a savior, or **messiah**, that would lead the Jews. A young Jewish man known as Jesus began to spread his ideas. Jesus' followers called him "Christ," which was based on the Greek word for messiah (Khristós). Christians are those who follow the teachings of Christ. Christians believe that Jesus is the son of God, and that he died for the sins of all people. Therefore, people who follow the teachings of Jesus and acknowledge him as the Son of God will be forgiven from their sins and enter Heaven after death.
>
> Directly south of Mesopotamia is the Arabian Peninsula. The inhabitants of that region were known as Arabs. Arabs believed they were descended from Abraham through another son, Ishmael. Arabs acknowledged the teachings of Judaism and Christianity, but the majority of Arabs worshiped various local gods. Around 600 CE in the city of Mecca, a young man named Mohammad began to share new ideas, or **revelations** from Allah (the Arabic word for God). Mohammad told the people of Mecca that Allah had given revelations first to the Jews, and then to the Christians. Mohammand was the final **prophet** (or messenger) and was tasked with sharing the final revelations from Allah. The revelations spread by Mohammad become the foundations for Islam, which means "submitting to the will of Allah." A follower of Islam is known as a Muslim.

1. What does the term "Christ" mean?

   A. Jesus' last name

   B. A follower of Jesus

   C. "Messiah"

   D. A carpenter

2. To Muslims, what is Mohammad's role in Islam?

   A. A savior

   B. A prophet

   C. A deity

   D. A political leader

**3.** In which region did Christianity and Islam orginate?

    **A.** Southwest Asia

    **B.** Southeast Asia

    **C.** South Asia

    **D.** East Asia

**4.** Think about the different religions mentioned in the text. What's one thing they seem to have in common? What's one way they seem different?

............................................................................................................................................

............................................................................................................................................

............................................................................................................................................

............................................................................................................................................

............................................................................................................................................

............................................................................................................................................

............................................................................................................................................

............................................................................................................................................

**CHRISTIANITY**

**ISLAM**

**Directions:** Read the text in the table below. Then answer the questions that follow.

| Belief System | Judaism | Christianity | Islam | Zoroastrianism |
|---|---|---|---|---|
| **Origin/ Founder/ Dates** | Abraham, Canaan (present-day Israel & Palestine), 1000s BCE | Jesus, Judea (present-day Israel & Palestine), 1st century CE | Mohammad, Mecca (present-day Saudi Arabia), 600s CE | Zarathustra/ Zoroaster, Persia (present-day Iran), 1000s BCE |
| **Basic Beliefs** | Yahweh's chosen people due to the covenant with Abraham. Obedience to God shown through multiple cultural practices throughout the year. | Jesus is the Son of God, sacrificed to forgive the sins of believers. Jesus died and was resurrected. He and his followers spread his teachings throughout the world. | Mohammad received the final messages from Allah. He was commanded to spread these revelations so that all may live according to the will of Allah. | Ahura Mazda and Ahriman are engaged in an eternal battle of light vs. dark, good vs. evil. By choosing good actions, believers support Ahura Mazda and will strengthen light (symbolized by fire) in the world. |
| **Current Global Distribution** | Due to fleeing persecution over the centuries, Jewish communities are found all over the world. The largest communities can be found in Israel, the United States, and many European countries. | Currently the largest religion, Christians live all over the world. | Currently the second-largest religion, the majority of Muslims are in the Middle East/ Southwest Asia, North Africa, South Asia, and Indonesia in Southeast Asia | With only 100,000 -200,000 followers today, clusters of Zoroastrians can be found in India, Iran, Iraq, and the United States. |

| Belief System | Judaism | Christianity | Islam | Zoroastrianism |
|---|---|---|---|---|
| **Importance of converting others** | Low. Jews believe they are descended from Abraham through Isaac, so family lineage is important. It is possible to convert Jewish practices, but can not convert to become a Jew. | High. Spreading the teachings of Jesus is an important part of practicing Christiantiy. | High. Spreading the revelations of Allah and the teachings of Mohammad is an important part of practicing Islam. | Low. To be considered Zoroastrian, a child must have two Zoroastrian parents, or at least a Zoroastrian father. There is some debate on this in modern Zoroastrianism. |

**1.** Which religion did not originate along the eastern coast of the Mediterranean Sea?

..............................................................................................................................

**2.** In what parts of the world will you find the majority of Muslims?

..............................................................................................................................

..............................................................................................................................

**3.** Which religion has the most practitioners today? ..............................................

**4.** Which two religions are the oldest? ..................................................................

**5.** Which two religions place an emphasis on spreading their faith and converting other people? ..............................................................................

**Directions:** Read the text below. Then follow the instructions to complete the activity.

In Week 5 you learned about the system of dates that are often used when studying history: the use of BCE and CE. Today you will learn about how centuries are measured.

A **century** is a period of 100 years. If something has existed for five centuries, that means it has been there for five hundred years. But when we refer to a specific century by number, it can get confusing. Look at the timeline below. You can see that the years following 0 are marked as the 1st Century CE, or first hundred years after 0.

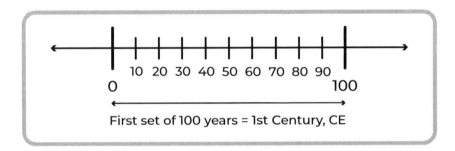

First set of 100 years = 1st Century, CE

But if you look at the actual years, the 1st century is actually the years 0-99. Take a look at how the timeline continues below.

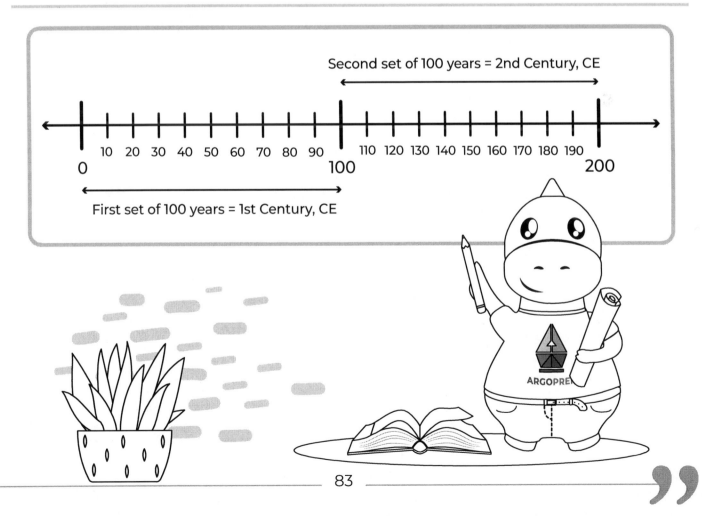

Second set of 100 years = 2nd Century, CE

First set of 100 years = 1st Century, CE

The 2nd Century CE is actually the years 100-199. Use the chart below to better understand the pattern.

| Century Number | Years #s in that Century |
|---|---|
| 3rd century | 200-299 |
| 4th century | 300-399 |
| 5th century | 400-499 |
| The pattern continues when you get into higher-numbered years | |
| 11th century | 1000-1099 |
| 12th century | 1100-1199 |
| 13th century | 1200-1299 |
| And continues to the present-day | |
| 19th century | 1800-1899 |
| 20th century | 1900-1999 |
| 21st century | 2000-2099 |

Sometimes historians don't know the exact year in which something happened, but they do know the general timeframe. So instead of saying the specific year, they'll give the centuries, often with a descriptive word like "early," "mid-," or "late."

"Christiany spread rapidly during the 3rd century CE"

"Buddhism began during the 6th century BCE."

"The number of people with cell phones grew rapidly in the early 21st century."

"Scientists hope to land humans on Mars by the beginning of the 22nd century."

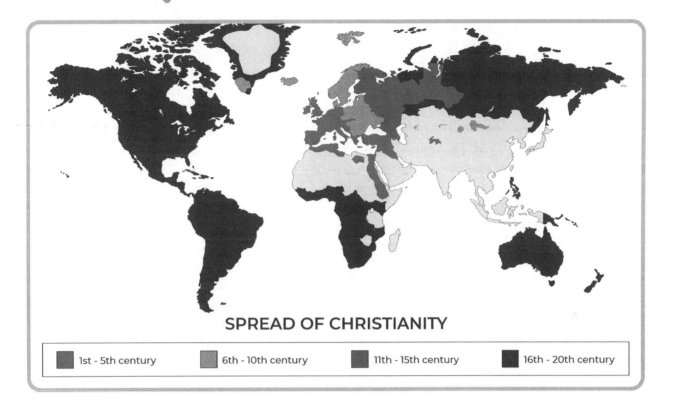

**SPREAD OF CHRISTIANITY**

| ■ 1st - 5th century | ■ 6th - 10th century | ■ 11th - 15th century | ■ 16th - 20th century |

**1.** In what century is the year 1492? ................................................................................................

**2.** What years make up the 10th century? ....................................................................................

**3.** During what range of centuries was Christianity introduced to the Americas?

...............................................................................................................................................................

**4.** Describe where Christianity spread during each span of 500 years. Use the maps from Week 1 and Week 2 to describe the locations.

| *Example:* During the 1st - 5th centuries CE, Christianity spread through the Middle East, along the Nile River, and around the Mediterranean Sea and southern Europe. |
| --- |
| |
| |
| |

**Directions:** Read the text below. Then complete the activity that follows.

As you learned last week, religions often hold many different things as "sacred." Believers have invested a lot of time and wealth into building and maintaining places of worship (such as temples for Jews, churches and cathedrals for Christians, mosques for Muslims, and temples for Buddhists). Many of these sacred buildings have existed for hundreds of years. These buildings are often excellent examples of the art and architecture of the cultures that live there. As a result, they are a draw for tourists who visit the region.

For many tourists, visiting an important religious location may be the only exposure they have to those religious beliefs. Learning about different beliefs can lead to more religious tolerance. However, having tourists in a sacred space can make it harder for a believer to focus on their prayers or rituals. This could lead to tension between visitors and believers.

In the space below, describe your thoughts on whether or not tourists should be allowed to visit sacred spaces. Do you think it is good for people to experience the sacred locations of other religions? Do you think it is fair for people who have come to worship to have tourists wandering around? How do you think this issue could be resolved?

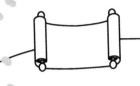

# WEEK 8

## Chinese Civilizations. Qin & Han

This week you will return to China to learn about the classical civilizations of the Qin and Han. This time period greatly increased Chinese influence in Asia.

ARGOPREP

**Directions:** Read the text below. Then answer the questions that follow.

In Week 5 you learned about the **dynastic cycle** and three of the early Chinese dynasties (Xia, Shang, and Zhou). This week we will study two of the dynasties that had an incredible amount of influence on China through to the present-day. These are the Qin Dynasty (226-201 BCE) and the Han Dynasty (206 BCE - 220 CE). Notice that the Qin Dynasty occurs before the date of 0 in the western calendar, and the Han Dynasty is split between BCE and CE.

As you may recall from learning about the dynastic cycle of Chinese history, a period of peace and stability during a dynasty was followed by a period of decline and fall. The first emperor, Qin Shi Huang, conquered the surrounding states and unified the core of what will be identified as China. Qin Shi Huang controlled the land along the Yellow River and Yangtzee River, and spread his rule further to the north and south. Therefore, although it was only a couple of decades long, the Qin Dynasty is recognized as having unified the region under one rule. It is believed that the English word for "China" comes from "Qin."

The Han Dynasty comes after the fall of the Qin. The Han Dynasty lasted for around 400 years. Confucianism becomes recognized as a specific set of beliefs and practices during this time. The stability during the Han Dynasty allowed for trade to spread around the region and a trade network known as the "Silk Road" flourished (this was not a specific road, but a series of interconnected trade routes). The Silk Road stretched from China in the east, through northern India and Persia, and reached the Roman Empire in the west. Major trading centers developed into cities, some of which still exist today. The Han Dynasty covered the same area as the Qin Dynasty, and extended it even further to the north, south, and west. The Han Dynasty lasted until the 3rd century CE.

1. What developed during the Han Dynasty that allowed trade to flourish?

   **A.** The Great Wall

   **B.** The Yangtze River

   **C.** The Yellow River

   **D.** The Silk Road

2. How long was the Han Dynasty?

   **A.** 426 years

   **B.** 206 years

   **C.** 201 years

   **D.** 226 years

3. Which of the following is true of the Han Dynasty?

   **A.** It was smaller than the Qin Dynasty

   **B.** It did not include part of territory controlled by the Shang.

   **C.** It was larger than the area controlled by Qin Shi Huang.

   **D.** It did not stretch beyond the Yangtzee River.

**Directions:** Read the text below. Then answer the questions that follow.

Both the Qin and the Han dynasties developed an autocratic government system (with power held by one person - in this case, an Emperor). The day-to-day actions of the government were run by a number of government workers. During the Qin Dynasty, a philosophy known as **Legalism** guided the legal and justice systems. The basic idea of Legalism is that humans are primarily selfish. If given the opportunity, they will do bad things like steal and kill. Therefore, there should be very severe punishments to discourage people from making bad decisions. There should also be rewards to encourage good behavior. This way, society will remain harmonious because people will choose good behavior and avoid doing bad things.

The severity of Legalism ultimately led to the Qin Dynasty's collapse. You may recall the role of the Mandate of Heaven played in the dynastic cycle. As people fought back against the Legalist consequences, civil unrest spread. Civil unrest is when people violently push back against something they disagree with as a form of protest. One of the characteristics of losing the Mandate of Heaven is civil unrest, so it provided an opportunity for someone else to step in and claim the Mandate, which the founders of the Han Dynasty did.

A couple of major changes were made to laws and government during the Han Dynasty. While Confucian ideas had existed for hundreds of years (remember, Confucius lived around 300 years earlier), it was during the Han Dynasty that it became the official ruling philosophy. One of the major changes was the idea that government jobs shouldn't just go to people who were wealthy and close to the emperor. Instead, they should go to the person who has the right knowledge and skills for the job. This is the idea of **merit**. A series of tests known as the **civil-service exam** helped identify people who were the best fit for the job. As a result, the importance of education increased during this era, as gaining a job in the government was a way to increase the social status of the worker's family.

The Han did not entirely abandon the Legalist philosophy of the Qin. However, the popularity of the merit system allowed Han rulers to remain in power for over 500 years.

**1.** What is the basic idea of Legalism?

   **A.** Humans can make good decisions

   **B.** Humans are selfish

   **C.** Humans should be given choices

   **D.** Humans can work together

2. What was the evidence that the Qin Dynasty was losing the Mandate of Heaven?

   **A.** Severe Legalist consequences
   **B.** Trade slowed down
   **C.** Multiple years of drought
   **D.** Civil unrest

3. What does "merit-based system" mean?

   **A.** Important jobs should be given to those close to the Emperor
   **B.** Family members should inherit jobs
   **C.** Jobs should go to those who are qualified for them
   **D.** Jobs should be a reward for skill in battle

4. Why was education important during the Han Dynasty?

........................................................................................................................

........................................................................................................................

........................................................................................................................

**Directions:** Read the text below. Then answer the questions that follow.

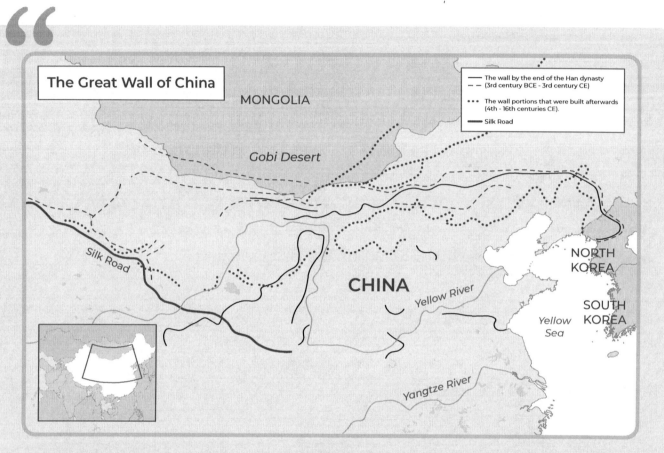

The Great Wall of China is one of the Seven Wonders of the World. The Seven Wonders are massive things built by people that can still be seen today (as opposed to the Seven Wonders of the Ancient World, most of which have been lost). The Great Wall has never been one continuous wall. It is a series of walls, towers, fortresses, shelters, and paths. It was built over hundreds of years to defend different parts of China from invasions that frequently came from the north. Each dynasty added to the wall and repaired older parts, or removed parts that were no longer necessary. The Qin emperor was the first to organize widespread construction and repair of many parts of the wall and is often described as having built the wall, but that is not entirely accurate. But he was responsible for strengthening it for future generations.

In 1987 the Great Wall of China was identified as a UNESCO World Heritage Site, which protects the wall from being destroyed or changed. According to UNESCO, the Great Wall of China is the only man-made structure that can be seen from the moon. While not the only wall that was built to keep out invaders, it is the only one in the world that was continually built and maintained for over 2000 years for the same purpose - to represent and preserve China and Chinese identity.

**1.** For what purpose was the Great Wall of China built?

.........................................................................................................................................

.........................................................................................................................................

**2.** Instead of being one single wall, the Great Wall of China is made up of what?

.........................................................................................................................................

.........................................................................................................................................

.........................................................................................................................................

.........................................................................................................................................

**Directions:** Read the text below. Then answer the questions that follow.

When a society has long periods of stability, it encourages people to spend time creating and exploring, instead of always being focused on surviving chaos. The Han Dynasty is an excellent example of this. While there was still fighting, especially on the northern borders, people during this time also had the ability to develop advancements in science, architecture, and technology, among many others.

The **seismograph** was a Han-era development that was used to record earthquakes that happened far away. It was also used to determine in what direction the earthquake happened. When earthquake waves were detected, a small ball rolled into the mouth of a frog. The earthquake came from the direction that the frog was facing.

Chinese horse riders developed a way to keep their legs close to the horse's sides. The **stirrup** allowed riders to use pressure from their legs and feet for better control over their own balance as well as for communication with their horse. This technology spread rapidly through the nomadic tribes to the north and will have a significant impact on trade and warfare for centuries to come.

**Paper** as we know it today was developed during the Han Dynasty. Chinese paper was made from soaking the bark of the mulberry tree, combined with old scraps of fabric and other fibers. After soaking, the mixture was pounded into a pulp, which was then poured through a screen and dried. Compared to papyrus, paper was more durable and easier to make.

Probably the longest-held secret in world history, the method for making **silk** was unknown outside of China for over 3,000 years. When processed correctly, threads from the cocoon of a moth can be woven into an incredibly strong yet soft fabric that was used in a variety of ways. Although the method for making silk had been known for thousands of years, it was during the Han Dynasty became a major trade good. It was also during this time that the secret to production made its way out of China.

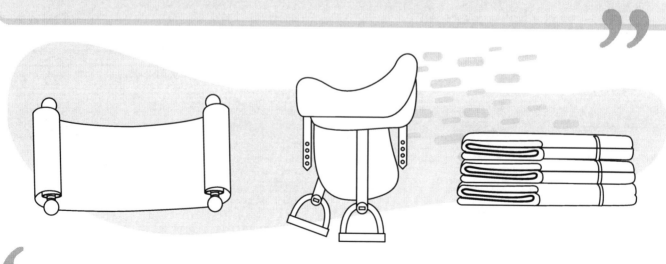

**1.** Why are technological advancements frequently developed during long periods of peace and stability?

.......................................................................................................................................................

.......................................................................................................................................................

.......................................................................................................................................................

**2.** What's a problem you've noticed that could use a new invention? Describe your idea for this invention. How would it work, and what challenges might you face in creating it?

.......................................................................................................................................................

.......................................................................................................................................................

.......................................................................................................................................................

.......................................................................................................................................................

.......................................................................................................................................................

.......................................................................................................................................................

.......................................................................................................................................................

**Directions:** Read the text below. Then complete the activity that follows.

This week you learned about the Chinese philosophy of Legalism. The idea that people need severe consequences in order to make better choices is not unique to ancient China. The concept continues today with the idea of deterrence. To "deter" means to redirect, or avoid something. In criminal justice, the idea of deterrence is that if the consequence of an action is severe enough, then people will avoid doing that action.

Legalism and deterrence both have the same root concept: Humans are inherently selfish and will act in their own interests. Governments throughout history have used a variation of this belief to maintain control over their citizens.

What do you think? Are humans inherently selfish? Do we do good things simply because we want to avoid a consequence? Can people do good things simply because they want to, without the expectation of some reward? In the lines below, record your thoughts to these age-old questions.

# Mediterranean Civilizations: Ancient Greece

This week you will learn about the origins and influence of ancient Greece on the civilizations of the Mediterranean Sea.

ARGOPREP

**Directions:** Read the text below. Then answer the questions that follow.

The present-day country of Greece is located in the Eastern Mediterranean. The geography of Greece is very mountainous and full of rocky coastlines and hundreds of islands. Due to the difficulty in traveling, Ancient Greece was made up of a number of independent and individual city states. Although they shared a common language and religion, each city state was fiercely independent and they engaged in frequent warfare. The people of Greece called this region "Hellas," and the time period is known as the Hellenic Era.

Two of the most famous city-states in Greece were Athens and Sparta. By 500 BCE, Athens had become the center of Greek culture. Art, literature, and music were all studied and appreciated there. It was the destination for anyone interested in learning and questioning. The study of **philosophy**, or "love of wisdom," was born in Athens. Philosophers would gather to discuss their ideas and listen to some of the most important thinkers in western civilization: Socrates, Plato, and Aristotle.

Sparta, on the other hand, developed into one of the strongest military societies of the ancient world. Both men and women in Sparta were trained to fight and defend. A famous battle against the mighty Persian Empire involved only 300 Spartans who held off thousands of Persian soldiers for three days. The Spartans were eventually betrayed and defeated by the Persians, but it allowed the rest of the Greek city-states to regroup for a series of battles to eventually push the Persians back out of Greece.

1. Why did the geography of Greece cause the development of independent city-states?

   **A.** The coastlines led to a lot of fishing

   **B.** People used resources from the mountains

   **C.** Athens was located in the north, and Sparta in the south

   **D.** It was hard to travel between city-states, so it kept them mostly separate from each other

2. What term do historians use to describe this period of Greek history?

   **A.** Hellenic Era

   **B.** Hellenic Dynasty

   **C.** The Greek Era

   **D.** The Athens & Sparta War

**3.** Socrates, Plato, and Aristotle were known as which of the following?

   **A.** Astronomers

   **B.** Philosophers

   **C.** Astrologers

   **D.** Cartographers

**4.** Describe what you think it would be like to grow up as a child in Athens compared to Sparta. What would you learn about? How would you be taught? What might you grow up to become?

| Life in Athens | Life in Sparta |
| --- | --- |
| | |

**Directions:** Read the text below. Then answer the questions that follow.

Although the Greek city-states were united against the Persian Empire, once the Persian threat was gone they returned to battling between themselves. Athens and Sparta continued to fight against each other, weakening both city-states and not paying attention to the actions of the northern region of Macedonia. The Macedonians greatly admired the accomplishments of the Greeks, but the Greeks saw them as inferior. In the 4th century BCE, a Macedonian king named Philip II (read as Philip the Second) improved upon Greek military tactics and began to move south into Greece. He conquered (or allied with) many of the city-states and ultimately took control. After his death in 336 BCE, his son Alexander became king of Macedonia and Greece.

Alexander the Great only ruled for 13 years (336-323 BCE) but the effects of his actions lasted for centuries. He had been trained by the most elite Greek teachers (his tutor was the Greek philosopher Aristotle). He was also highly trained in military tactics. Over the next eleven years, he conquered the rest of Greece, Egypt, Mesopotamia, Persia, and continued moving east until he and his men reached the Indus River. As they conquered a region, Alexander established cities (often bearing his name) and put loyal Greeks in charge. He also put Greeks in charge of existing cities. As Alexander's army moved east, Greek language and culture followed.

This era was known as the Hellenistic Era. Hellenistic means "Greek-like" because although it was based on Greek culture, there were many changes that happened as people from distant places interacted. Long after Alexander was gone, the influence of Greek culture would continue. This had a huge impact on trade and communication, as trade goods and information (such as technology and religious beliefs) could be exchanged along the existing trade routes. The Mediterranean world was now a major participant in Silk Road trade.

After Alexander and his army reached the Indus River, his men were ready to stop fighting. They were faced with two options: They were going to rebel, or they would turn around and head back to Greece. He decided to listen to his men, but took a more northern route which allowed him to establish control over a much larger region. Alexander the Great died in 323 BCE in the Mesopotamian city of Babylon, without ever returning to Greece. After his death his empire was divided up between his generals. Greek language and culture continued to thrive in the region. It also merged with local cultures to create unique cultural fusions.

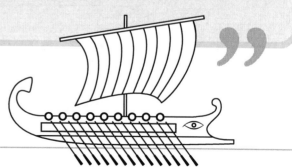

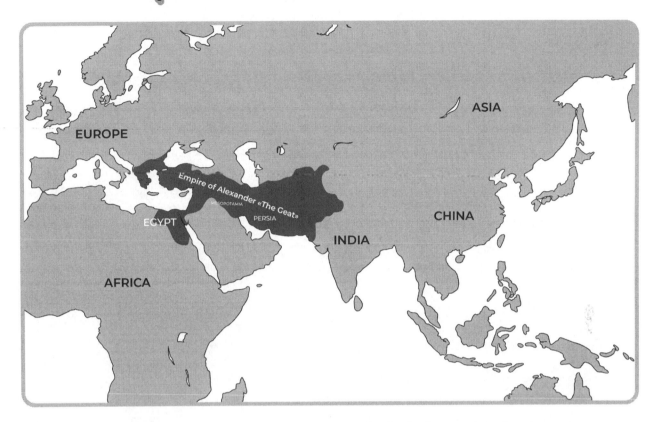

**1.** What name is used to describe the time period of Alexander the Great's conquests and the centuries that followed?

  **A.** The Alexandrian Era      **C.** The Persian Era

  **B.** The Hellenic Era      **D.** The Hellenistic Era

**2.** Where was Alexander originally from?

  **A.** Greece      **C.** Babylon

  **B.** Persia      **D.** Macedonia

**3.** Which of the following is not a region that was conquered by Alexander the Great?

  **A.** China

  **B.** Mesopotamia

  **C.** Greece

  **D.** Egypt

**4.** Why did Alexander **not** continue to push into India?

  **A.** He was killed in Babylon

  **B.** His men refused to continue pushing east

  **C.** His generals took over his empire

  **D.** He was defeated by the Spartans

**Directions:** Read the text below. Then answer the questions that follow.

So far, we have discussed one type of leadership: an autocracy, where power is held in the hands of a single individual, such as a king (in a monarchy) or an emperor (in an empire). Another form of government developed during Ancient Greece where the people had the power.

The Greek word for "people" is demos. The suffix "-cracy" means power. Put those two roots together and you get Democracy! In a democracy, decisions are made by the people through citizen involvement - voting. There are two types of democracy. The city of Athens was known for the first type we will be studying: Direct Democracy.

Male citizens of Athens were able to vote directly on the laws that were proposed. Once a law was introduced, people had the opportunity to ask questions, debate, and discuss the possible issues. They were then able to vote in favor of or against the law. Since individuals were able to vote directly on laws, this was known as Direct Democracy. This system works well in a small population where people have the ability to be involved. As we will see next week, challenges arise as the population grows.

The founders of the United States government had studied the Greek form of democracy. We can find examples of Direct Democracy in local and statewide elections. For example, when a law has been proposed, the information is published in a booklet for people to review. There are meetings where people can discuss the pros and cons of the law, and citizens can then vote directly on the law on Election Day.

**1.** If you could make one new rule for your school or neighborhood, what would it be and why? What might be one good result and one possible problem from this rule?

........................................................................................

........................................................................................

........................................................................................

........................................................................................

........................................................................................

........................................................................................

**Directions:** Read the text below. Then complete the activity that follows.

Athens was known by all to be the center of learning in Ancient Greece. Many of the topics you will study in high school and college were first explored during this time. As a result, the words that we use in math, science, medicine, law, and many other subjects originally came from Greek words. Studying Greek (and Latin) root words will be very helpful when learning more complex words. Often, what appears to be a long, scary word is actually just two or three roots put together. If you know what the roots mean, you can make a pretty good guess as to the meaning of the word!

| Greek root | Meaning | English word |
|---|---|---|
| bio | life | Biology - the study of life |
| -ology | study of | |
| micro | small | Microscope - (tool) to see small things |
| scope | to see | |
| poly | many | Polytheistic - belief in many gods |
| theo | god | |
| demos | people | Democracy - people have the power |
| -cracy | power | |
| sub | under | Submarine - (ship) under the sea/water |
| mar/mer | sea/water | |

Do an internet search for "Greek & Latin Root Words" or find a larger dictionary. Look up the roots below, combine the meanings, and see if you can figure out what English word they create. Write down the English word and what it means. The first one has been done as an example. Be aware - many of the words have more than one meaning. Try a few different combinations to find one that makes sense!

| Root Word | English Meaning | English Word & Meaning |
|---|---|---|
| auto | self | Autobiography - a book written by a person about their own life |
| bio | life | |
| graph | write | |
| mono | one | |
| chrom | color | |
| micro | | |
| bio | | |
| -ology | | |
| syn | | |
| nym | | |
| homo | | |
| phone | | |

**Directions:** Read the text below. Then follow the instructions to complete the activity.

Stories about the Greek gods & goddesses have fascinated people for centuries. Similar to Egypt and Mesopotamia, the Greeks were polytheistic and worshiped gods that were connected to various aspects of nature. Greek writers also documented detailed and elaborate stories about the gods' interactions with other gods as well as with humans. As a result, we are also able to see how Greek culture (and religious beliefs) changed over time. While much of the upper classes could read and write, the majority of the population was illiterate. Greek stories were shared orally (spoken out loud) and passed down through the generations. Different versions of the stories were eventually written down.

## Ancient Greece Gods/Goddesses

| Name | Role (what are they God or Goddess of?) | Symbol (what symbol is associate with the God or Goddess?) |
|---|---|---|
| **Zeus** | King of the Gods God of the Sky | Thunderbolt |
| **Hera** | Queen of the Gods | High Crown |
| **Athena** | Goddess of War and Cunning Wisdom | Owl |
| **Apollo** | God of the Sun, Truth, Music, Poetry, Dance, and Healing. | Bow (during war) Lyre (in peace) |
| **Demetra** | Goddess of Fertility and Agriculture | Sheaves of Grain |
| **Poseidon** | God of the Sea and Horses | Trident |
| **Aphrodite** | Goddess of Love and Beauty | The Dove |
| **Hermes** | God of Travel, Business, etc. Mescencer God | Traveler's hat, winged sandals, staff |

| Name | Role (what are they God or Goddess of?) | Symbol (what symbol is associate with the God or Goddess?) |
| --- | --- | --- |
| **Artemis** | Goddess of Hunting, Archery, Childbirth Goddess of the Moon | Bow and Arrow |
| **Ares** | God of War | Armor and Helmet |
| **Hephaestus/ Hephaistos** | God of Fire, Volcanoes, Blacksmiths, and Craftspeople | Tools/Twisted Foot |
| **Hades** | God of the underworld | Invisible Helmet |

**1.** Have you seen or read stories about any of these gods? Describe where you've seen/read about them, and what you recall.

.......................................................................................................................................

.......................................................................................................................................

.......................................................................................................................................

**2.** How can an oral storytelling tradition lead to slightly different versions of a story?

.......................................................................................................................................

.......................................................................................................................................

.......................................................................................................................................

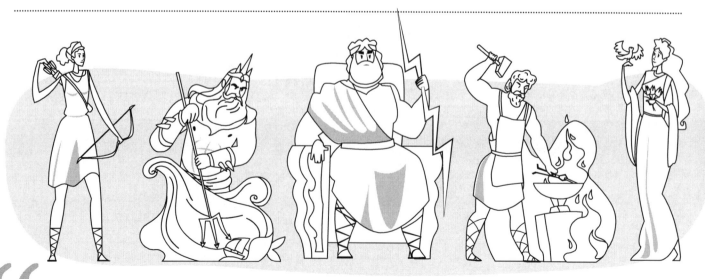

# WEEK 10

# Mediterranean Civilizations - Ancient Rome

This week you will learn about the influence of ancient Rome on Europe and the Mediterranean, as well as long-term effects globally.

ARGOPREP

**Directions:** Read the text below. Then answer the questions that follow.

Greece maintained its dominance over the Eastern Mediterranean until around 200 BCE. While Alexander the Great was spreading Greek influence to the east, another group was consolidating their power in the west. The city of Rome is located in present-day Italy. A group who spoke the Latin language began to conquer their neighboring communities. Over the next 700 years, Rome would grow from a small farming village to an empire that surrounded the entire Mediterranean Sea and set the foundation for much of Western Civilization.

The secret to Rome's success was their adaptability. They borrowed ideas and technology from the people they conquered and adapted those ideas into even more impressive achievements. For example, the Persians had mastered the technology of making roads that stretched for a thousand miles. The Romans utilized that technology to build more permanent roads in order to transport troops to distant locations and spread Roman control. The roads also helped to expand trade (and taxation) opportunities. They also mastered the **arch**, which enables architects to design taller structures. The arch was used to build **aqueducts**, which allowed them to bring in water from mountains that were hundreds of miles away. This led to the growth of massive cities, such as the capital of Rome.

From the Greeks they adopted democracy, religion, and language, and then adapted them into something different. Greek gods became Roman gods with Latin names. Greek words and linguistic elements were incorporated into Latin and spread throughout the empire. Military tactics from defeated armies were incorporated into the Roman military. Successful soldiers were given land in the growing empire, so the military was strengthened with eager volunteers. Over 400 years, Rome would grow to one of the great empires of world history.

**1.** What language did the Romans speak and spread?

    **A.** Latin          **C.** Italian

    **B.** Macedonian    **D.** German

**2.** Which of the following was **not** adopted from the Greeks?

    **A.** Roads          **C.** Religion

    **B.** Language      **D.** Government

**3.** Where is the city of Rome located?

    **A.** Present-day Greece      **C.** Present-day Iraq

    **B.** Present-day Egypt       **D.** Present-day Italy

**4.** The Romans were successful due to which of the following characteristics?

    **A.** Copying and duplicating

    **B.** Adopting and adapting

    **C.** Creating and discovering

    **D.** Destroying and discarding

**Directions:** Read the text below. Then answer the questions that follow.

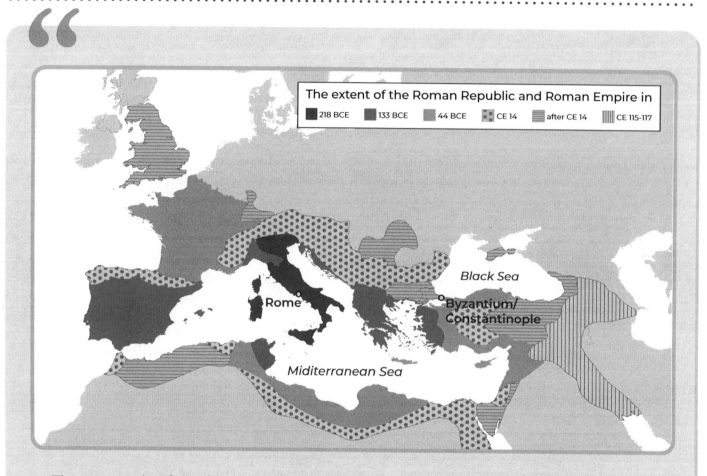

The extent of the Roman Republic and Roman Empire in

218 BCE | 133 BCE | 44 BCE | CE 14 | after CE 14 | CE 115-117

Black Sea

Rome

Byzantium/
Constantinople

Miditerranean Sea

The strength of the Roman military and road system allowed Roman control to spread throughout the Mediterranean Sea, Europe, North Africa, Egypt, and parts of the Middle East. Rome reached its greatest extent in the 2nd century CE. After that, the territory under Roman control would begin to shrink. During the 4th century the empire was split into two parts: The Western Roman Empire with the capital at Rome, and the Eastern Roman Empire with the capital at Byzantium. Soon after, the city was renamed Constantinople after the emperor Constantine.

The Roman Empire in the west began to crumble in the 5th century. The empire in the East, which would become known as the Byzantine Empire, would continue to flourish for another thousand years. We will learn about both of these empires in future weeks.

1. Which of the following was **not** part of the Roman Empire (use a modern map if needed).

   **A.** France

   **B.** Italy

   **C.** Spain

   **D.** Ireland

2. Which body of water was completely surrounded by the Roman Empire?

   **A.** The Black Sea

   **B.** The Atlantic Ocean

   **C.** The Pacific Ocean

   **D.** The Mediterranean Sea

3. Use a modern map to find the names of four present-day countries that were once part of the Roman Empire.

   **A.** ........................................................................................................

   **B.** ........................................................................................................

   **C.** ........................................................................................................

   **D.** ........................................................................................................

4. What challenges do you think the leaders of Rome faced as the empire expanded?

.........................................................................................................

.........................................................................................................

.........................................................................................................

.........................................................................................................

.........................................................................................................

.........................................................................................................

.........................................................................................................

.........................................................................................................

**Directions:** Read the text below. Then answer the questions that follow.

One of the most recognizable buildings of the Mediterranean world is the Roman Colosseum. Built nearly 2,000 years ago, the Colosseum has withstood war, earthquakes, and scavenging. Despite the damage it has sustained, the Colosseum still gives us an excellent example of the architectural genius of Roman architects and builders.

The Colosseum was built during the 1st century CE as a gift from the emperor to the people of Rome. It hosted gladiatorial games, mock battles (it was even flooded to include ships!), and public executions. It could hold 50,000 people at a time, and was designed so all of those people could exit the building in less than ten minutes.

Eventually, the events at the Colosseum began to lose popularity. Over time, many of the decorations and good-quality building materials were removed and recycled into other building projects. The Colosseum we see today is actually just the internal structure of what it once was.

While the Colosseum fascinates people for its bloody history and visual appeal, there's actually one building that is still in near-perfect condition and is still being used for its original purpose. Built between the 1st and 2nd century CE, the Pantheon was used as a place to worship all of the Roman gods, as opposed to being dedicated to just one god. When Rome adopted Christianity as the official religion in the 4th century it became a Christian place of worship, and that has continued through to the present day.

In addition to the Roman arch, they also mastered the technology of the dome. The Pantheon has no internal support; the weight of the ceiling rests on the outer walls. The hole in the ceiling is actually the only source of light. When it rains, the water flows down into grates in the floor. Legend says that the Renaissance painter and architect Michelangelo actually removed a piece of the Pantheon's dome to try to figure out how it was built. Many of the architectural techniques used in the Pantheon are still being discussed today.

Historians consider these types of buildings to be "monumental architecture." They are built to not only serve a specific purpose, but to also show off the power and wealth of the society. The goal is for people to be so impressed with the skill and cost of such a massive structure, that it acts as a deterrent to invasion. They want people to think "If they are wealthy enough to build this, then they must have a very powerful army as well! We better not try to defeat them!" In addition, leaders want to shock and impress their own people. These structures are probably the largest and most impressive buildings that they will ever see - more proof that they are part of an incredibly powerful society.

**1.** Have you ever visited somewhere that was large or memorable in some other way? What did you see? How did it make you feel? How would you describe it to a friend who will be going there soon?

........................................................................................................................

........................................................................................................................

........................................................................................................................

........................................................................................................................

........................................................................................................................

........................................................................................................................

........................................................................................................................

........................................................................................................................

........................................................................................................................

........................................................................................................................

**Directions:** Read the text below. Then answer the questions that follow.

The government of the United States is based on two forms of democracy. Last week you learned about the Greek system of direct democracy, which is when people can vote directly on laws. Today we will discuss the Roman contribution to the system.

As you may recall, direct democracy works well in small populations, and in small areas. But, as populations grow, it becomes much more difficult to be an active participant in the process. Just traveling to the voting location would be a challenge. Think about it: In order for the United States to have a true direct democracy, every voter would need to be able to travel to Washington D.C. for every vote. Considering that the United States government passes hundreds of laws a year, this would not be realistic.

Ancient Rome had the same challenge. Look back at the map from Day 2. Some parts of the empire are hundreds of miles away from Rome. So instead of having everyone vote on everything, people voted on people to act as **representatives**. The representatives would then travel to Rome to make decisions based on what the people wanted. This is known as a **republic** or a **representative democracy**. Representatives are elected to represent the people.

Today, the United States has a combination of direct democracy and representative democracy. Some of our local laws are voted on by the people directly. Some of our leaders are also voted on directly by the people such as state governors. But we also vote for representatives to vote on our behalf at the local, state, and national level. The system of government in the United States, even though it is only just over 200 years old, has its roots in ancient Greek and Roman democracy.

**1.** Who is the governor of your state? When were they elected? Ask someone who voted in the last election some of their thoughts on the democratic system of the United States.

..................................................................................................................................

..................................................................................................................................

..................................................................................................................................

..................................................................................................................................

..................................................................................................................................

..................................................................................................................................

**2.** In 1-2 brief sentences, describe the difference between direct and representative democracy.

................................................................................................................

................................................................................................................

................................................................................................................

................................................................................................................

**3.** Why was it difficult for ancient Rome to use a direct democracy system? How does this relate to the United States today?

................................................................................................................

................................................................................................................

................................................................................................................

................................................................................................................

................................................................................................................

................................................................................................................

**Directions:** Read the text below. Then answer the questions that follow.

> As you read in week 8, Christianity began in present-day Israel. 2,000 years ago, that region was under the control of the Roman empire. Christianity was initially forbidden by the Romans. Rome had adopted and adapted (and changed the names of) the polytheistic gods from Greece. In addition, some of the emperors demanded to be worshiped as a god. In contrast, Christianity was a monotheistic religion - there was only one god, and it wasn't Jupiter (Zeus) or the emperor!
>
> Christianity grew slowly over time, but by around 300 CE it had become much more popular. The mother of the Emperor Constantine was a Christian, and in 313 CE he declared that all religions, including Christianity, were allowed. A few decades later it was adopted as the official religion of Rome. The city of Rome became the center of the Christian church.
>
> The government of Rome eventually split into two parts in the 4th century. Since many religious practices had also become part of government actions, the religion also split in two. The city of Rome became the center of the Roman Catholic Church. The city of Byzantium (later Constantinople) became the center of the Byzantine, or Eastern Orthodox Church. Eventually, the two branches of Christianity would develop different practices and beliefs that continue to this day. However, they both believe in the role of Jesus as messiah, or savior, and are therefore both still considered part of Christianity.

**1.** Why was Christianity considered illegal prior to the 4th century CE?

.........................................................................................................................................................

.........................................................................................................................................................

**2.** When and how did Christianity become legal in Rome?

.........................................................................................................................................................

.........................................................................................................................................................

**3.** Why are the Catholic Church and the Orthodox Church both considered part of the Christian faith?

.........................................................................................................................................................

.........................................................................................................................................................

# Comparing Classics

This week you will analyze similarities and differences between the civilizations of China and the Mediterranean.

ARGOPREP

**Directions:** Read the text below. Then answer the questions that follow.

The past few weeks have focused on the classical civilizations of the Mediterranean Sea and the rivers of eastern China. This week will be focused on comparing those two important regions.

The chart below has a variety of characteristics that are found in civilizations throughout history. The term **characteristic** refers to the major topics that we study when learning about history: things like religion, economy, social structure, government systems, etc. Each civilization has those things, but each of those characteristics looks different. When we learn about a new place, we use the details of these characteristics as a way to compare them.

For example, we can examine the characteristic of "belief systems" to see how they are similar or different. "Belief systems" is a characteristic that both regions have, but the specifics of those belief systems are different (the Mediterranean is focused on worshiping a specific god, whereas in China the focus is more on behaving appropriately to keep things stable. With each characteristic, you can find things that are both similar and different.

Review what you have learned in the previous chapters. In the chart below, add additional information about each characteristic on the left. You will use this information on Day 3.

| Characteristic | Mediterranean | China |
|---|---|---|
| Belief Systems | | |
| Writing/Record Keeping | | |
| Major Cities | | |
| Government | | |

**1.** Characteristics are things that can be compared between two or more things. Which of the following are examples of a characteristic?

   **A.** Clothing styles

   **B.** Traditional foods

   **C.** Music

   **D.** All of the above

**2.** Which of the following is a specific similarity between the two civilizations?

   **A.** In both regions, major cities developed by large bodies of water.

   **B.** They both have government systems.

   **C.** They have different languages.

   **D.** They both developed writing systems.

**3.** What is a major religious difference between the two regions?

   **A.** They developed religions at different times.

   **B.** One developed Buddhism while the other developed Christianity.

   **C.** The Western religions focused more on worshiping a specific god, while the Eastern religions focused on maintaining stability.

   **D.** They both had emperors who ruled.

**CHRISTIANITY**          **BUDDHISM**

**Directions:** Answer the questions that follow.

A. Using maps from previous weeks, or from other sources, locate the greatest extent of each of the Classical civilizations we have studied: Greece & Rome in the Mediterranean, and Qin & Han in China.

B. Color each civilization in a different color and create a key in the space in the corner.

C. Label all rivers.

1. At its largest, which civilization controlled the most territory (land and water)?

   **A.** Greece          **B.** Qin          **C.** Rome          **D.** Han

2. Which civilization controlled the most coastline?

   **A.** Greece          **B.** Qin          **C.** Rome          **D.** Han

3. Which civilization controlled the least amount of territory?

   **A.** Greece          **B.** Qin          **C.** Rome          **D.** Han

4. Which civilization controlled the most major rivers?

   **A.** Greece          **B.** Qin          **C.** Rome          **D.** Han

**Directions:** Refer to the chart on Day 1. Fill in the sentence frames to make comparative statements.

Similarity statements:

Example: Both <u>Rome</u> and <u>Han China</u> had <u>several major cities.</u>

**1.** Both ............................................ and ............................................ had

............................................................................................................................

**2.** Both ............................................ and ............................................ had

............................................................................................................................

Difference statements:

Example: Although <u>Rome and China both developed major cities</u>, <u>Roman cities often developed along the coastline</u> while <u>Chinese cities developed along rivers.</u>

**1.** Although ........................................................................................................ ,

........................................................................................................ while

............................................................................................................................

**2.** Although ........................................................................................................ ,

........................................................................................................ while

............................................................................................................................

**Directions:** Read the text below and follow the instructions provided to complete the activity.

> Similar to the Chinese dynastic cycle, civilizations rise and fall in a cyclical (circle-like) pattern. Often a civilization will have a period of peace, stability, and prosperity. During these times, people are able to focus on things other than warfare and survival. While there may still be conflict, especially along the borders, the majority of the inhabitants experience a **period of peace**. **Stable governments** during this time encourage an increase in trade which leads to **economic growth**. Since fewer people are needed to support a constant military presence, more people can devote time to **art, music**, **literature**, and **technological advancements**.

Each of the following statements is a description of a civilization during what historians often consider to be their Golden Era. For each description, identify which Golden Era characteristic can be identified.

> Greece: "...the magnitude of our city draws the produce of the world into our harbor, so that to the Athenian the fruits of other countries are as familiar a luxury as those of his own." -Thucydides "History of the Peloponnesian War"

**1.** Which characteristic of a Golden Era can be found in this quote?

A. Art & Music

B. Science & Technology

C. Stable Government

D. Trade & Economic prosperity

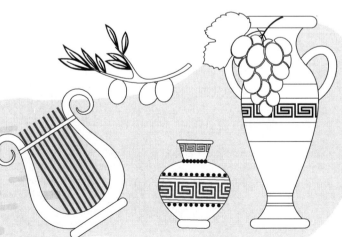

> Rome: "As far as peace is concerned the people have no need of political activity, for all war, both Greek and foreign, has been banished and has disappeared from among us." -Plutarch, "The Blessings of Imperial Rule: Peace and Prosperity"

**2.** Which characteristic of a golden era can be found in this quote?

**A.** Peace

**B.** Science & Technology

**C.** Trade & Economic Prosperity

**D.** Stable Government

> China: "He who exercises government by means of his virtue [goodness] may be compared to the north polar star, which keeps its place and all the stars turn toward it." -Confucius, "The Analects"

**3.** Which characteristic of a golden era can be found in this quote?

**A.** Art & Music

**B.** Science & Technology

**C.** Stable Government

**D.** Trade & Economic prosperity

**Directions:** Read the text below and follow the instructions provided to complete the activity.

> Both China and the Mediterranean world had periods of peace and prosperity, as well as warfare and conflict. One of the similarities between the two regions is that they had golden eras at approximately the same time in history.

1. What is a golden age, and what evidence can be found to support the idea of a golden age in China and the Mediterranean?

......................................................................................................................

......................................................................................................................

......................................................................................................................

......................................................................................................................

......................................................................................................................

......................................................................................................................

......................................................................................................................

......................................................................................................................

......................................................................................................................

......................................................................................................................

......................................................................................................................

......................................................................................................................

......................................................................................................................

......................................................................................................................

......................................................................................................................

......................................................................................................................

# Europe in the Middle Ages

This week you will learn about Europe after the fall of the Roman Empire, an era known as the "Middle Ages."

ARGOPREP

**Directions:** Read the text below. Then answer the questions that follow.

> As you learned in Week 10, the Roman Empire grew too large to manage, and was divided into two regions: The Western Roman Empire with its capital in Rome, and the Eastern Roman Empire with its capital in Byzantium. We will be learning about the Byzantine Empire in Week 13. For this week we will focus on the Roman Empire in the west. The Middle Ages are divided into three major eras: the Early Middle Ages (sometimes referred to as the Dark Ages), the High Middle Ages, and the Late Middle Ages.
>
> One of the challenges that the Roman Empire constantly faced was with attacks along the borders from various nomadic tribes. As the Roman Empire began to weaken, these tribes were increasingly successful in breaking through the fortifications and reaching Roman cities. During the 4th and 5th centuries CE, a number of tribes known as Goths raided Roman cities throughout the empire. To the Latin speakers of the Roman Empire, these groups spoke languages that sounded like repetitions of the syllable "bar," and were collectively called "**barbarians**." In 476 CE a group of barbarians sacked the city of Rome and took control. This event was part of the slow decline of Roman authority in Europe, and is the traditional date that historians use to mark the fall of Rome.
>
> Over the next 400 years, nomadic groups continued to move into the cities. Starting in the 9th century, overcrowding in the far northern region of Scandinavia led to invasions by the Norsemen (also known as **Vikings**). In addition to Viking invasions, Europe in the 9th - 11th centuries was engaged in constant internal conflict. Trade and travel slowed to a trickle, and most people never traveled farther than 10 miles from the village in which they were born. Leaders built up massive fortifications, known as **castles**, to protect their cities and resources. Very few people were able to read and write, so records from this time period are very limited. This era is often known as "the **Dark Ages**," not because all of it was bad, but because we are so limited on what we know about it.
>
> The continent began to stabilize in the 10th and 11th centuries, although regional warfare was still very common. But the majority of military action shifted to the Middle East during this time. The Crusades dominated European military and politics for the next few hundred years.
>
> Throughout this time, the **Catholic Church** solidified its hold on the continent in both religion and politics.
>
> Another key event of the Middle Ages was the **Black Death** or **Black Plague**. A mysterious and deadly illness swept through the continent. There was no cure, and no one at the time knew what caused it or how it spread. Scientists have since determined that it was caused by bacteria that spread through the air and through person-to-person contact. Hygiene and sanitation were nonexistent during the Middle Ages,

"

so the disease was able to quickly spread through communities. Over the span of about five years, over 50% of the population died.

The late 1300s through the 1500s are characterized by a renewed interest in the Greek and Roman eras. Greek & Roman writings (which had been preserved by Muslim libraries in Baghdad and other Middle Eastern cities as well as in Muslim Spain), were reintroduced to the European elite. The achievements of Greece & Rome were seen as the "**Classical Era.**" The **Renaissance**, or "rebirth" was a reawakening of the classical era. Therefore, the centuries in the middle were simply an era between the two "enlightened" eras. This is where the term "**Middle Ages**" comes from. The Classical Era is from the 6th century BCE to the 5th century CE. The Renaissance begins in the 14th century CE. The Middle Ages are roughly the thousand years between Greece & Rome and the Renaissance. The term "**medieval**" is often used to describe the Middle Ages. Medieval is simply the English version of the Latin term for middle ages, and is used as an adjective (for example, medieval warfare = warfare of the Middle Ages.)

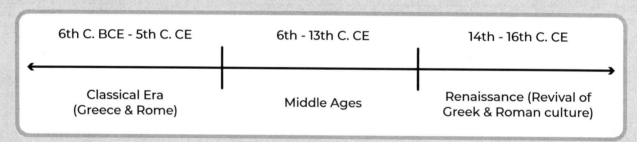

| 6th C. BCE - 5th C. CE | 6th - 13th C. CE | 14th - 16th C. CE |
|---|---|---|
| Classical Era (Greece & Rome) | Middle Ages | Renaissance (Revival of Greek & Roman culture) |

"

**1.** The word "medieval" refers to the

   **A.** Middle World    **B.** Middle Ages    **C.** Meditation    **D.** Medium

**2.** The Vikings invaded Europe from which direction?

   **A.** North    **B.** East    **C.** South    **D.** West

**3.** Approximately how many years are part of the Middle Ages?

   **A.** 100    **B.** 300    **C.** 500    **D.** 1000

**4.** The Middle Ages are called that because they are between which two eras?

   **A.** The Renaissance and the Modern Age

   **B.** The Classical Era and the Renaissance

   **C.** The Age of Exploration and the Renaissance

   **D.** The Classical Era and the Roman Empire

**Directions:** Read the text below. Then answer the questions that follow.

> During the Middle Ages, Europe was fragmented into dozens, if not hundreds, of competing political groups. Small areas were controlled by whomever was strong enough to defeat their opponents and then maintain that territory. There was a lot of political chaos. But there was one organization that maintained its hold over European civilization despite the political fragmentation that surrounded it: the Christian Church.
>
> Christianity began during the Roman Empire, and spread along its shorelines and trade routes until it was the dominant religion in Europe. Once the Roman Empire split, the church did as well. In the west, the Christian church was centered in the city of Rome. You will recall that one of the reasons for Christianity's popularity was that anyone could become a Christian. It is considered a "universal" religion, and the word for universal in Greek can be translated as "catholic." Therefore, the Christian church that continued in the west is known as the Roman Catholic Church, the Catholic Church, or just the "Church" (with a capital C). When writing about the religion of this time period, historians will use these three terms interchangeably.
>
> Religion was incredibly important to people in the Middle Ages. Due to the political chaos of constantly warring kingdoms, threats of invasion by barbarian tribes and the constant threat of sickness, famine, and natural disasters, the Church was often the only form of stability. People's lives revolved around two things: agriculture and religious events. Religious leaders (known as **clergy**) were responsible for guiding the people (the **laity**, or those who were not religious leaders) through their life on Earth so that they could go to Heaven after death. In exchange for spiritual guidance, people were expected to give part of their income to the church. This was the cycle that led to the continuation and stability of the Catholic church: the laity provided for the needs of the clergy (food, supplies, money, etc.), and the clergy provided for the spiritual needs of the laity (baptisms, Communion, weddings, funerals, etc.). Therefore, even though people in different parts of Europe spoke different languages and had different political leaders, they all shared in one "universal" religion.

**1.** Which of the following is a group of religious leaders?

    **A.** Laity

    **B.** Clergy

    **C.** Fealty

    **D.** Vassal

**2.** Which of the following is used to describe the religious organization centered in Rome?

    **A.** Roman Catholic Church

    **B.** Catholic Church

    **C.** The Church

    **D.** All of the above

**3.** When studying religion, what does the term "universal" mean?

    **A.** The study of space

    **B.** Something that is available to anyone

    **C.** Only available to some

    **D.** The study of the ocean

**4.** What role did the clergy play in this system?

    **A.** They provided for the religious needs of the community

    **B.** They organized the military of the region

    **C.** They provided food, clothing, etc. to the religious leaders

    **D.** They voted on the laws as representatives of the people

**Directions:** Read the text below. Then answer the questions that follow.

> The social and political structure of the European Middle Ages is known as **feudalism**. During the European Middle Ages, all land in a particular region was controlled by an autocratic leader known as a king. In order to maintain control over large areas, a king would have his nobles swear an oath of loyalty, or **fealty**, to him. By swearing fealty, the noble would become a **vassal** of the king and would be considered a lord over a chunk of the king's land. In exchange, it was expected that the king would provide for the defense of the overall land, or **kingdom**.
>
> The land under the control of the vassal was known as a **fief** or **fiefdom**. In order to maintain law and order in the fiefdom, the lord would gather vassals of his own to swear fealty to him (and, by extension, the king). Each vassal would provide to their lord (their "landlord") a portion of the goods and agricultural products produced within the fief. Vassals were also required to provide **knights** to their lord in the event of conflict. Knights were warriors who swore fealty to the region's lord. Knights were sometimes holders of their own small fiefdoms, or they were hoping to be awarded with land after successful service in battle.
>
> The king, nobles, vassals, and knights made up part of the upper levels of the medieval social structure. As you may recall from Day 2, the Catholic Church had a similar structure that existed alongside the political ones. It was a complicated relationship. While the lord had political authority over the bishop, for example, the bishop had spiritual authority over the lord. It was believed that going against the religious guidance of the Church could risk the lord's ability to go to Heaven after death. As a result, the Catholic Church maintained a lot of political and religious power in Europe
>
> At the bottom of the social scale were the **peasants** and **serfs**. Generally, peasants and serfs were responsible for the day-to-day duties of keeping the fiefdom running. They were responsible for farming, crafting, building, and any other tasks that needed to be done. The peasants & serfs had very few rights or protections, but were essential to the long-term success of the fief.
>
> A peasant was considered a "freeman," which meant that (theoretically) they had the freedom to live where they wanted or do a job that they wanted. A serf, on the other hand, was bound to the land. That meant that whoever controlled the land in that region also controlled the actions of the serfs. In reality, both peasants and serfs lived a life of hard work with little reward, and were the foundation of the entire **feudal system**.

**1.** Which of the following is a nobleman who controls the land?

    **A.** Lord                     **C.** Serf

    **B.** Peasant                **D.** Fief

**2.** Which of the following is a person who has sworn fealty to the king?

    **A.** Feudal                **C.** Vassal

    **B.** Fief                    **D.** Serf

**3.** Which of the following is a gift of land to use?

    **A.** Feudal                **C.** Vassal

    **B.** Serf                   **D.** Fief

**4.** Which of the following best describes the term "fealty"?

    **A.** Family

    **B.** Loyalty

    **C.** Agriculture

    **D.** Belief

**Directions:** Read the text below and follow the instructions provided to complete the activity.

After the fall of Rome and increase in barbarian invasions, it became incredibly unsafe to travel. Even though Rome had established an efficient network of roads, eventually those roads were primarily used by warring armies as opposed to merchants and messengers. Trade and travel trickled to a near standstill, and people lost contact with others outside their region.

The Latin language had spread along with Roman culture and religion. But as people stopped interacting, each isolated region became its own mini "language island." Languages change over time; ask an adult about the types of words they used with their friends when they were younger, and how those words compare to how you talk today. After nearly 1,000 years, the language that had previously been spoken all over Europe had evolved into dozens of individual and distinct languages.

The present-day languages of Italian, Spanish, Portuguese, Romanian, and French (among others) all developed from Latin. These languages are often referred to as "Romance" languages because they came from the language spoken by those in Rome. In this context, *"Romance"* does not refer to a love story, but instead the languages that developed from what was spoken by the Romans.

English, on the other hand, is descended from two very different languages. The Romans reached England during the 2nd century CE, however they were only able to maintain control there for about 200 years before drawing back into France. The language spoken by the majority of people in England was a Germanic language, brought there by tribes who migrated from present-day Germany. The two most populous tribes were the Angles and the Saxons.

In the year 1066 CE, William of Normandy (or William the Conqueror), crossed the English Channel and defeated the English king. The French-speaking Normans took over as the nobility in the region. French then became the language of learning, education, wealth, power, law, etc. The Anglo-Saxon peasants and serfs continued to speak their Germanic languages. But over the next few hundred years, the languages spoken in England evolved into one primary language: English, which has roots in both German (from the Anglo Saxons) and Latin (from the French spoken by the Normans).

| English | book | bread | family | friend | well/good |
|---|---|---|---|---|---|
| Latin | liber | panem | familia | amicus/ amica | bene |
| Italian | libro | pane | famiglia | amico/ amica | bene |
| French | livre | pain | famille | ami/amie | bien |
| Spanish | libro | pan | familia | amigo/ amiga | bien |
| Portuguese | livro | pão | família | amigo/ amiga | bem |
| Romanian | carte | päine | familie | prieten | bine |
| German | buchen | brot | familie | freund | gut |

**1.** In addition to the words in the chart above, what other words do you know that came from a different language, or sound similar in another language? Try to think of 3-4 words and their origins.

........................................................................................................

........................................................................................................

........................................................................................................

........................................................................................................

**2.** Have you studied another language? Have you ever traveled somewhere where a language was spoken that you did not understand? Describe that experience here. If you have not experienced another language, describe what you think it would be like and how you would respond.

........................................................................................................

........................................................................................................

........................................................................................................

........................................................................................................

**Directions:** Read the text below and follow the instructions provided to complete the activity.

This week you learned about the European Middle Ages - from the fall of Rome to the dawn of the Renaissance. For each day this week, write 1-3 sentences that summarize the topic. In the last box, draw a picture to illustrate something you found interesting about the European Middle Ages.

**1.** Fall of Rome & Overview.

........................................................................................................................

........................................................................................................................

........................................................................................................................

**2.** The Catholic Church.

........................................................................................................................

........................................................................................................................

........................................................................................................................

**3.** Feudalism & the Medieval Social Structure.

........................................................................................................................

........................................................................................................................

........................................................................................................................

**4.** European Languages.

........................................................................................................................

........................................................................................................................

........................................................................................................................

........................................................................................................................

**Directions:** Illustration of something from the European Middle Ages.

# WEEK 13

# The Spread of Islam

This week you will learn about the rapid expansion of the religion of Islam.

ARGOPREP

**Directions:** Read the text below. Then answer the questions that follow.

As you learned in Week 7, Islam began in present-day Saudi Arabia with the prophet Muhammad sharing the revelations he received from Allah. Within 100 years after his death, Islam grew to cover the majority of the Middle East and stretched into north Africa and parts of central Asia. The rapid spread was due to both military conquests as well as voluntary conversion - there were economic and spiritual benefits to practicing Islam.

After Muhammad's death in 632 C.E., his followers appointed a new religious leader, or **caliph**. The first four caliphs were men who had traveled with Muhammand and were responsible for gathering the revelations of Allah into the **Quran**, the holy text of Islam. But there was disagreement as to who would become the leader of Islam; Muhammad did not name the person who would be in charge as his **successor**. Some Muslims believed that the caliphs should be chosen by the community. This group is known as Sunni Muslims. Others felt that the caliph must be from Muhammad's family line. They are known as **Shi'a** Muslims. The two branches of Islam split early on and the division continues to the present day.

The first major expansion of Islam was under the Umayyad Caliphate. From 661-750, northern Africa, southern Spain, and the majority of the Middle East (most of present-day Türkiye was controlled by the Byzantines). They also spread to the east and conquered the Persian Empire.

The Umayyads were overthrown in 750 by the Abbasids, who established the Abbasid Caliphate. The Abbasids moved the capital to Baghdad, in modern Iraq, and expanded Muslim rule into Central Asia. The Abbasids ruled until the city of Baghdad was sacked by the Mongols in 1258. By the 16th century, the majority of the Middle East fell under the control of the Ottoman Empire, which lasted until the end of World War I in the early 1900s.

1. In which century did Islam begin?

   **A.** 4th          **B.** 5th          **C.** 6th          **D.** 7th

2. Who or what is a caliph?

   **A.** A religious leader          **C.** A sucessor to Muhammad
   **B.** A political leader          **D.** All of the above

3. In what year did the Mongols sack the city of Baghdad?

   **A.** 1066          **B.** 1099          **C.** 1258          **D.** 1479

**Directions:** Read the text below. Then answer the questions that follow.

The religion of Islam is practiced by millions of people around the world. The cultures of each region have influenced how the religion is practiced in each area. There are some core parts, however, that remain consistent across all believers.

The **Five Pillars of Islam** are the core beliefs and practices of all Muslims. The chart below describes each of the five pillars. In addition, the Arabic language unites believers through the text of the Quran. The classical Arabic version is used in religious ceremonies, so many people learn it as part of their religious study.

| Shahadah | Salat | Zakat | Sawm | Hajj |
|---|---|---|---|---|
| Statement of Faith | Daily Prayers - 5 times per day | Giving charity to support the poor and needy | Fasting during the month of Ramadan | Making the pilgrimage to Mecca at least once |

One of the unifying features of Islam is the expectation that all Muslims make the pilgrimage to Mecca at least once in their life. Muslims from all over the world travel to present-day Saudi Arabia to participate in the rituals and practices of the hajj. By participating in religious ceremonies alongside people from other cultures, the hajj provides an opportunity to learn about and appreciate people from diverse cultures who are united through a shared faith.

**1.** Participation in the annual feast month of Ramadan is known as

    **A.** Zakat          **B.** Salat          **C.** Sawm          **D.** Hajj

**2.** The Hajj is the pilgrimage to which Muslim holy city?

    **A.** Medina

    **B.** Mecca

    **C.** Riyadh

    **D.** Jeddah

**3.** The statement of faith is the

    **A.** Hajj

    **B.** Sawm

    **C.** Zakat

    **D.** Shahadah

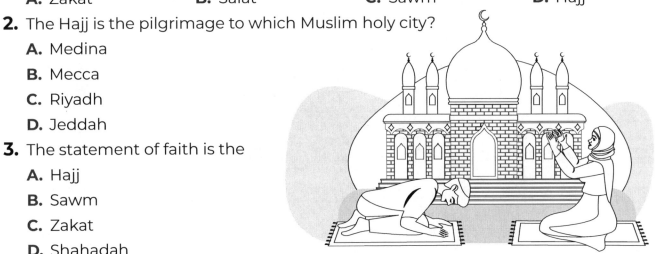

**Directions:** In the space below, create a timeline of the spread of Islam. Use the dates listed in the key and the names of the various locations to provide detail to your timeline.

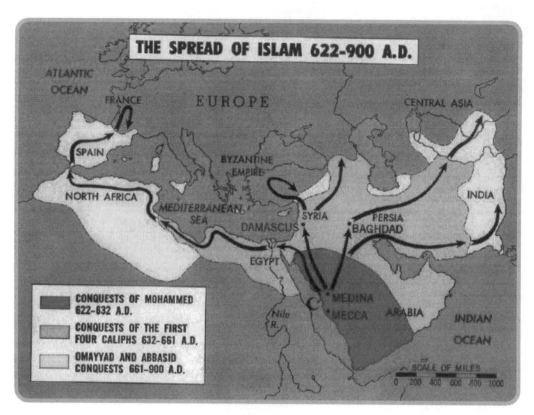

THE SPREAD OF ISLAM 622-900 A.D.

ATLANTIC OCEAN

FRANCE

EUROPE

CENTRAL ASIA

SPAIN

BYZANTINE EMPIRE

NORTH AFRICA

MEDITERRANEAN SEA

SYRIA

DAMASCUS

PERSIA

BAGHDAD

INDIA

EGYPT

Nile R.

MEDINA

MECCA

ARABIA

INDIAN OCEAN

CONQUESTS OF MOHAMMED 622-632 A.D.

CONQUESTS OF THE FIRST FOUR CALIPHS 632-661 A.D.

OMAYYAD AND ABBASID CONQUESTS 661-900 A.D.

SCALE OF MILES
0 200 400 600 800 1000

600 CE

1200 CE

**Directions:** Read the text below. Then answer the question that follow.

> As one of the Five Pillars of Islam, recognition of the holy month of Ramadan is a significant part Islamic worship. The timing of Ramadan changes each year and is based on the lunar calendar. During this time, Muslims do not eat or drink from sunrise to sunset. After the sun goes down, families and communities gather together to eat, celebrate, and give thanks. This month-long observation is another major unifying feature of global Islam.
>
> "The Islamic month of Ramadan is here, and I am excited by the calmness and reflection that this month brings. Ramadan, the ninth month on the Islamic calendar, is considered the holiest month for Muslims. It is a time where we fast, not just from eating food, but also from our worldly desires including things like shopping, or watching television — it's a time very similar to that of Lent for Christians. This month is dedicated to feeding our souls through reading more, praying more, and being more patient and kind to everyone, while attaching ourselves more to God. It is a month that is dedicated to spiritually grooming yourself to be a better person for the rest of the year..." Imani Bashir in Teen Vogue

**1.** Why does the global observance of Ramadan bring Muslims together as a community?

**Directions:** Read the text below and follow the instructions provided to complete the activity.

"

Two major centers of learning developed in the Islamic world. The Abbasid capital of Baghdad (in present-day Iraq) was the center of learning for much of the world at the time. After being overthrown, the Umyaads fled to the west and established the city of Córdoba in southern Spain. The 800s - 1200s are often considered the golden age of Islam.

The **astrolabe** was a device that allowed a ship to determine its latitude (how far north or south it was from the equator). The astrolabe would have long-term effects as it was used for future oceanic expeditions in both the eastern and western hemispheres.

**Algebra** is the mathematical study of finding an unknown number based on the information that you have. This, plus the use of Indian and Arabic numerals, had a significant impact on the study of mathematics.

Many works in Greek and Latin made their way to Baghdad and Córdoba, where they were translated into Arabic and studied. During the chaos of the fall of the Roman empire, a significant amount of **classical Greek & Roman writings** were preserved as a result of this translation and study. Later, the classical writings would be reintroduced to Europe and help fuel the Renaissance of the 14th century.

A number of advancements in **medicine** happened in the Islamic world. Muslim doctors understood that many diseases were infectious (as opposed to being a punishment from God) and established hospitals where people with similar symptoms were kept separate from others to avoid the spread of disease. Numerous surgical tools were developed and are still in use today.

Muslim tradition did not allow artists to create human forms in religious art. So **Islamic art and architecture** focused on the use of Arabic calligraphy (especially passages from the Quran) and geometric designs. Muslim buildings were decorated with intricate, multi-colored designs and the characteristic "horseshoe arch."

"

The 8th to 12th centuries are considered the Golden Age of medieval Islamic culture. Using examples from this week, write a paragraph that supports this statement.

........................................................................................................................

........................................................................................................................

........................................................................................................................

........................................................................................................................

........................................................................................................................

........................................................................................................................

........................................................................................................................

........................................................................................................................

........................................................................................................................

........................................................................................................................

........................................................................................................................

# WEEK 14

## The Byzantine Empire and the Crusades

 This week you will learn about what happened to the eastern part of the Roman Empire, and the conflict between Christian and Muslim armies during the 11th-14th centuries.

ARGOPREP

**Directions:** Read the text below. Then answer the questions that follow.

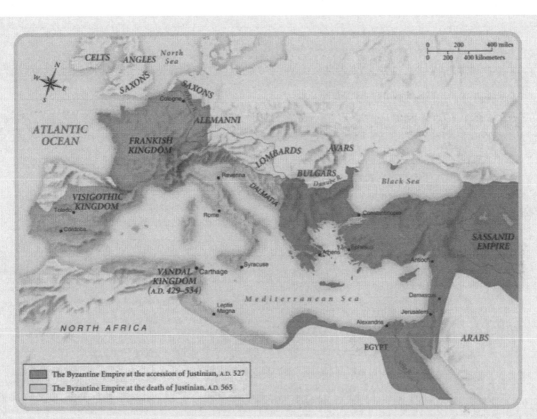

The Byzantine Empire at the accession of Justinian, A.D. 527
The Byzantine Empire at the death of Justinian, A.D. 565

After the fall of the Roman Empire in the west, the empire in the east continued to flourish for another thousand years. The capital city of Byzantium (Constantinople) sits at the crossroads of Europe and Asia through a major waterway that connects the Black Sea to the Aegean and Mediterranean Seas. Control over trade via water and land made the Byzantine Empire very powerful.

The Byzantine Empire further established Christianity as a major religion in the region. Differences in how the religion should be practiced led to a split (or **schism**) in 1054 between the Roman Catholic Church in the west and the Eastern Orthodox (or Byzantine) Church in the east. The city of Constantinople became the center of the Byzantine Church.

While geography protected the city of Constantinople, the rest of the empire was not as fortunate. After some initial reclaiming of areas around the Mediterranean that were previously controlled by Rome, the Byzantines would spend much of the next centuries trying to maintain control over its borders. Muslim forces eventually conquered Jerusalem, Damascus, and Antioch along the east coast of the Mediterranean sea, which would set the stage for the **Crusades**, a series of military conflicts between Christian and Muslim armies during the 11th - 14th centuries.

> The Byzantine Empire continued to struggle with both internal and external conflict through the 15th century. In 1453 the city of Constantinople was finally defeated by the Ottoman Turks, and the final remnant of the Byzantine Empire came under the control of the Ottoman Empire. Constantinople was renamed **Istanbul** and continues to be an incredibly important city in the region.

1. Which branch of Christianity was established in Byzantium?

    A. Catholic

    B. Protestant

    C. Orthodox

    D. Sufi

2. The location of Byzantium/Constantinople is important because

    A. It connects Africa to Asia

    B. It connects Europe to Africa

    C. It connects Asia to the Indian subcontinent

    D. It connects Europe to Asia

3. What empire eventually defeated the Byzantines?

    A. The Ottoman Empire

    B. The Abbasid Empire

    C. The Persian Empire

    D. The Mauryan Empire

**Directions:** Read the text below. Then answer the questions that follow.

By the beginning of the 11th century, most of the Middle East and parts of the Byzantine Empire had been conquered by Muslim armies or converted to Islam. This was seen as a threat to both religion and economics (trade) in Europe. Alexius I, the Byzantine Emperor, requested aid in the form of a small, highly-trained army, to help in Byzantine defense. Instead of granting that request, 1095, Pope Urban II in Rome called for the Christian countries of Europe to send their armies to the holy city of Jerusalem on a **crusade** (a noble mission) to "reclaim" those lands. In exchange, the Pope promised **remission** (forgiveness) of sins and direct entry into Heaven if they died during battle.

Kings, lords, vassals, and knights from all across Europe joined the cause and marched towards Jerusalem. They were accompanied by peasants and serfs as well, for the promises of the Pope were greatly desired. The cities along the way were unprepared for such a large, disorganized army and conflicts were frequent. Three years after they set out, the Crusaders finally took Jerusalem in a bloody battle with thousands of civilian deaths. The goal of the Crusade was achieved, but the costs were high.

> The leaders of the Crusade established control over territories in the region, known as Crusader States. These states were not long-lasting, as Muslim rulers pushed back in the years following. Over the next two centuries, the entirety of the Middle East returned to Muslim control. A number of additional Crusades were launched, although none of them had a long-lasting impact. The most significant effects of the Crusades were the reestablishment of travel and trade and an increase in the power and wealth held by the Roman Catholic Church. The weakened Byzantine Empire held on for another two hundred years but was ultimately defeated by the Ottoman Empire in 1479.

**1.** Who was the leader of the Byzantine Empire at the beginning of the Crusades?

   **A.** Pope Urban II

   **B.** Alexius I

   **C.** Saladin

   **D.** Henry III

**2.** The Crusaders could best be described as

   **A.** A disorganized collection of European nobles and commoners

   **B.** A highly-trained military

   **C.** A collection of elite soldiers

   **D.** Tourists

**3.** Who was the pope who encouraged Europeans to go on crusade?

   **A.** Pope Urban II

   **B.** Alexius I

   **C.** Saladin

   **D.** Henry III

**Directions:** Use the maps above to answer the following question.

### Mediterranean world after the First Crusade

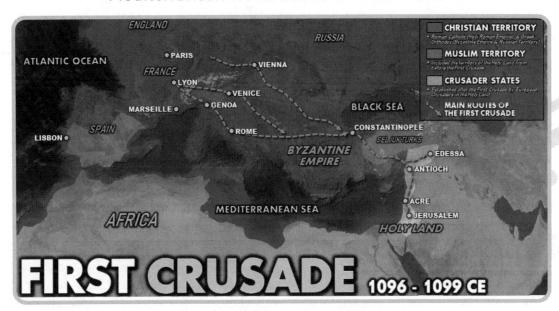

### Mediterranean world after the later crusades

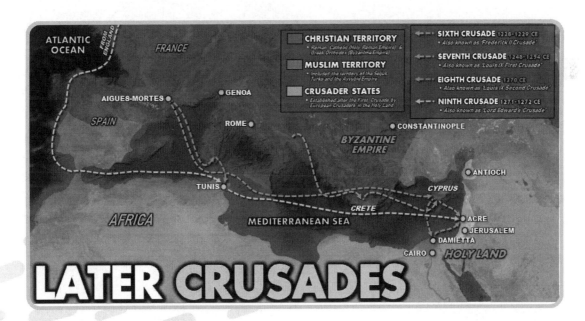

1. Which regions ended up under the control of a different group as a result of the Crusades? For each region, use the map to identify who controlled the region before and after the crusades.

........................................................................................................................

........................................................................................................................

........................................................................................................................

........................................................................................................................

........................................................................................................................

........................................................................................................................

........................................................................................................................

........................................................................................................................

........................................................................................................................

**Directions:** This map shows the global distribution of the major world religions, as well as where different branches of each religion are clustered. Use a modern map and this map to answer the following questions.

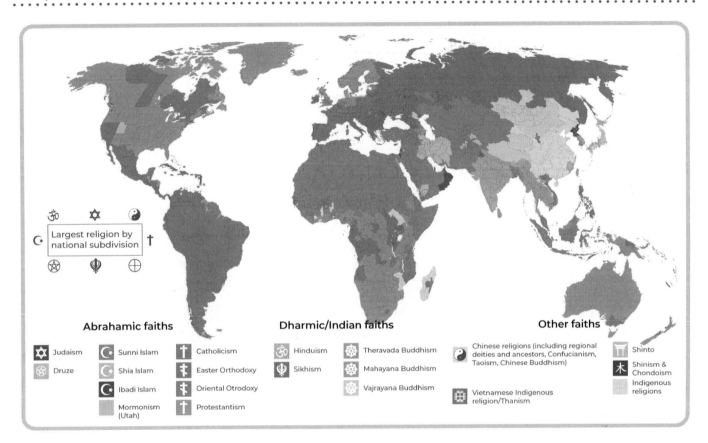

1. In what present-day countries will you find the majority of people practice Shia Islam?

   **A.** Egypt      **B.** Pakistan      **C.** Iraq      **D.** Lebanon

2. Which branch of Christianity is primarily practiced in South America?

   **A.** Roman Catholicism      **C.** Eastern Orthodoxy

   **B.** Protestantism          **D.** None of the above

3. The continent of Africa is primarily divided by which two religions?

   **A.** Islam & Buddhism       **C.** Judaism & Hinduism

   **B.** Hinduism & Christianity  **D.** Christianity & Islam

4. How many branches of Buddhism are shown in this map?

   **A.** One         **C.** Three

   **B.** Two         **D.** Four

**Directions:** In the Venn diagram below, write characteristics of each major religion. If the characteristic is shared by religions, write it in the overlapping areas of the circles. If the characteristic is unique to the religion, write it in its own area of the circle.

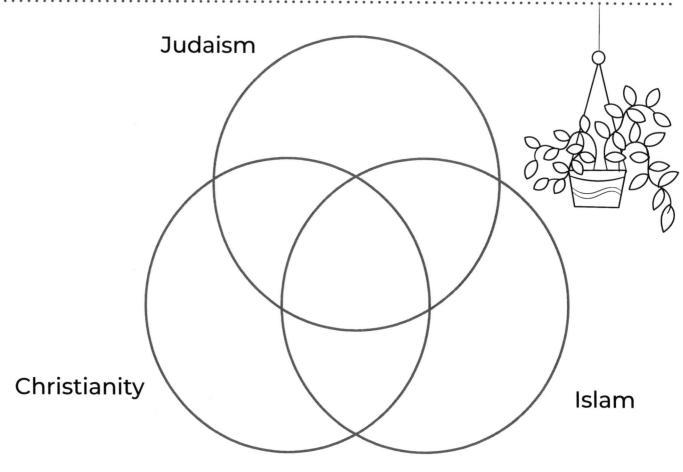

Judaism

Christianity

Islam

**1.** What is one thing that all three religions share?

...........................................................................................................................

...........................................................................................................................

**2.** What is one thing that is shared by two of the religions?

...........................................................................................................................

...........................................................................................................................

**3.** What is one thing that is unique about each of the religions?

...........................................................................................................................

...........................................................................................................................

# WEEK 15

# Indian Influences

This week you will return to India to learn about Indian social structure, history, and contributions to science, technology, and religion.

ARGOPREP

**Directions:** Read the text below. Then answer the questions that follow.

In Week 4 you learned about the ancient civilization of the Indus River Valley. Located in present-day Pakistan along the Indus River, the Indus River Valley civilization laid the foundation for much of Indian culture. While historians do not have a clear answer regarding what happened to the people of the Indus River Valley, there is evidence that many people migrated to the east and settled along the Ganges River.

Around the same time, groups of people from central Asia moved south. The combination of these two groups led to the development of early religious and historical texts known as the **Vedas**, and this era is known as the Vedic period. The Hindu religion became more formalized during this time. A social system also emerged, with religious leaders at the top, followed by warriors, peasants, and foreigners and laborers at the bottom. This system would develop over time into the rigid **caste system**.

For much of Indian history, small kingdoms battled with neighboring rulers for dominance over the land. In the 4th century B.C.E. much of the region came under the control of the **Mauryan** Empire. One of the Mauryan emperors, Ashoka, adopted the relatively new belief system of Buddhism and greatly supported its spread along existing trade routes. The Mauryan Dynasty ended in 185 B.C.E.

The Indian subcontinent was ruled by multiple groups over the next few hundred years, until the **Gupta** Empire emerged in the 4th century C.E. The Gupta emperors were primarily Hindu, however other religious beliefs were tolerated. Many scientific and mathematical advances occurred during the Gupta Dynasty, and many historians consider it to be India's "Golden Age."

The religion of Islam reached India during the 8th century C.E. Many trade routes were dominated by Muslim merchants. Many government leaders and wealthy families converted to Islam for religious as well as economic reasons. However, Hinduism continued to be the religion of the majority of the population. Two empires during the Muslim era were the Delhi Sultanate and the Mughal Empire. It was also during this time period that the religion of Sikhism developed.

By the 16th century, many European countries entered the Indian Ocean trade network. The distant British Empire established a presence in India and would exert control over the region through direct and indirect rule for 200 years. The nationalist movements of the 20th century led to the independence of India and Pakistan.

**1.** The Vedic Period is known for the development of what?

A. Islam

B. Hinduism

C. Daoism

D. Sikhism

**2.** What grew under the reign of the emperor Ashoka?

A. The caste system

B. The Vedas

C. Buddhism

D. Islam

**3.** During which era was India primarily controlled by Muslims?

A. The Vedic Period

B. The Gupta Dynasty

C. The Mauryan Dynasty

D. The Mughal Empire

**4.** Which Indian religion developed in the 15th century C.E.?

A. Sikhism

B. Buddhism

C. Jainism

D. Zoroastrianism

**Directions:** For the following questions, refer to the map above as well as other maps in this book.

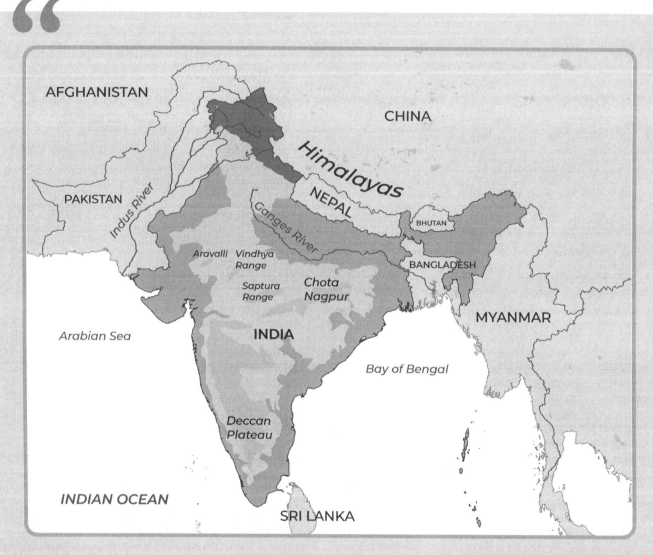

Like any other civilization, the history of India is heavily influenced by its geography. India is bordered on the north by mountain ranges, primarily the Himalayas. It is often referred to as a "subcontinent" because it is geographically separated from the surrounding areas. To the west lies the Arabian Sea, and the Bay of Bengal is in the east. The northern part is made up of the fertile regions of the Indus River, Ganges River, and many others. In the central and southern parts is the Deccan Plateau, a region with higher elevation and a drier climate than the rest of the subcontinent.

1. If someone were on the Deccan Plateau, in which direction would they travel to reach the Arabian Sea?

   A. North

   B. East

   C. South

   D. West

2. The mouth of which river can be found in the north of the Bay of Bengal?

   A. Indus

   B. Ganges

   C. Narmada

   D. Krishna

3. Which country lies between India and China (Tibet)?

   A. Pakistan

   B. Bangladesh

   C. Myanmar

   D. Nepal

4. In which region of India would you expect to find the largest population? Explain your answer.

   ..............................................................................................................................

   ..............................................................................................................................

   ..............................................................................................................................

   ..............................................................................................................................

**Directions:** Read the text below. Then answer the questions that follow.

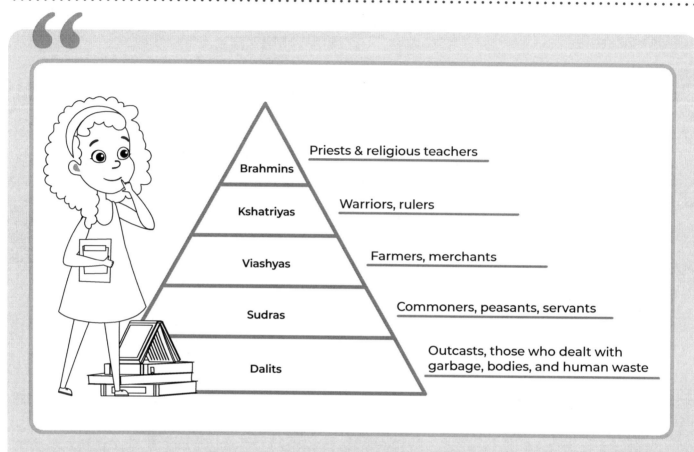

- Brahmins — Priests & religious teachers
- Kshatriyas — Warriors, rulers
- Viashyas — Farmers, merchants
- Sudras — Commoners, peasants, servants
- Dalits — Outcasts, those who dealt with garbage, bodies, and human waste

In Week 2 you learned about how social structures developed as people settled into agricultural societies. The system that developed in India (and endured for thousands of years) is known as the **caste system**. Each level, or jati within the system designated the types of jobs a person could hold, who they could marry, and their level of power and wealth within society. In general, it was not possible to move into a different caste; one's birth determined the caste.

The caste system was connected to society and religion. The social roles can be seen by the types of jobs that were available at each level. But the religious connection explains why the system has endured for so long. One of the core beliefs in Hinduism is the idea of karma, or the energy generated by a person's actions during their life. A person who generates good karma will be rewarded by being reborn at a higher level in the next life. A person with bad karma would be reborn at a lower level. The justification for the caste system is that the reason people were born at high/middle/low levels was based entirely on the karma they had generated in their previous life. And the only way to move up in the next life was by generating good karma - through fulfilling one's duty at home and in society.

> Many people, especially the Dalit, or those outside of the caste system, have dealt with extreme discrimination. During the era of British rule, historians argue that the caste system became more rigid and led to increased suffering of the Dalit and those at the lower levels. The Constitution that was developed during the Indian independence movement forbids caste discrimination, but many centuries-old practices continue.

**1.** Which level in the caste system is made up of farmers and merchants?

    **A.** Kshatriyas             **C.** Viashyas

    **B.** Sudras                **D.** Brahmins

**2.** What determined one's placement within the caste system?

    **A.** Karma                **C.** Jati

    **B.** Reincarnation       **D.** Sudras

**3.** Which group has experienced extreme discrimination as a result of the caste system?

    **A.** Brahmins

    **B.** Kshatriyas

    **C.** Jati

    **D.** Dalits

**Directions:** Read the text below. Then complete the activity that follows.

Despite thousands of languages and writing systems spoken around the world, one set of symbols is nearly universally understood: 0 - 9. Even in cultures whose writing systems record those numbers differently, the symbols of 0 through 9 are still frequently used.

There is debate over when the concept of zero as a specific number was established. What we do know is that it was used in writings by the Indian scholar Brahmagupta in the 7th century C.E. (The Mayans of central America independently developed the concept of zero around 600 years earlier, but it was primarily used in dates and calendars, not mathematics). The concept of zero is important because it allows for computations of larger and larger numbers. It also allows for an understanding of positive and negative numbers as well as imaginary numbers. Almost everything you interact with on a daily basis, from computers, to architecture, to space travel, relies upon the concept of zero.

In addition to the concept of zero, Indian mathematics gives us the shapes that we recognize as numbers. The Sanskrit numbers used in India traveled through the Arab world where they were modified to fit Arabic writing styles. They then moved into Europe and settled on their current shapes around 500 years ago.

| | | | | | | | | | | |
|---|---|---|---|---|---|---|---|---|---|---|
| Brahmi | | — | = | ≡ | + | 𑁖 | 𑁗 | 𑁘 | 𑁙 | 𑁚 |
| Hindu | ० | १ | २ | ३ | ४ | ५ | ६ | ७ | ८ | ९ |
| Arabic | ٠ | ١ | ٢ | ٣ | ٤ | ٥ | ٦ | ٧ | ٨ | ٩ |
| Medieval | o | I | 2 | 3 | Ջ | ϥ | 6 | ʌ | 8 | 9 |
| Modern | 0 | 1 | 2 | 3 | 4 | 5 | 6 | 7 | 8 | 9 |

**1.** Look at the progression of numbers in the chart above. Other than zero, which number looks the most like the original?

........................................................................................................

........................................................................................................

........................................................................................................

**2.** Which number has changed the most?

........................................................................................................

........................................................................................................

........................................................................................................

**3.** Why do you think the shape of the numbers changed as it moved through different eras and cultures?

........................................................................................................

........................................................................................................

........................................................................................................

**Directions:** Read the text below.

"

Many influential belief systems have emerged from one of the oldest and most populated regions of the world. Today you will learn a little more about the symbols found in the four main Indian religions: Hinduism, Buddhism, Jainism, and Sikhism. The symbols are all orange due to the color's sacred associations within India.

### Hinduism

**Symbol:** "Aum" or "Om"

**Origin:** Sanskrit language

**Significance:** Believed to be the sound of creation and the universe

### Buddhism

**Symbol:** Dharmachakra, or Wheel of Law

**Origin:** Also used in Hinduism, but with a different meaning

**Significance:** Represents the Buddha's teachings and the path to Enlightenment and Nirvana

### Jainism

**Symbol & Significance:** The **outline** is the shape of the Jain universe. The **dots** represent the different realms of existence, the **swastika** is an ancient Hindu symbol used to represent the four possible existences in Jainism, the **hand** symbolizes nonviolence, or ahimsa, the **circle** in the middle of the hand represents the cycle of rebirth, and the **24 spokes** within the circle are the 24 Tirthankaras, or guides to liberation.

### Sikhism

**Symbol:** The Khanda

**Significance:** The **vertical sword** is the khanda, representing truth or knowledge. The **circle** is the chakar, representing the endlessness and perfection of God. The **two swords** on the sides are, representing the responsibility to both religion and society.

"

**Directions:** Respond to one of the following questions.

A. If you follow an organized religion, does your religion have a symbol? If so, what does it look like, and what does it mean? If it has multiple parts, include a description of each part.

B. Choose one of the four symbols above. Using the internet or a history text, learn more about the symbol and write what you've learned in the space below.

# WEEK 16

# China & the World

This week you will examine ways in which Chinese influence in Asia has shaped the modern world, through language, politics, and technology.

ARGOPREP

**Directions:** Read the text below. Then answer the questions that follow.

> As you learned in Week 8, the Qin and Han Dynasties united much of China for the first time. After the fall of the Han Dynasty in the 3rd century, China faced three hundred years of political conflict. Buddhism entered China during this time, as the combination of political fragmentation and invasions from northern "barbarians" led many to question the Confucian ideals of their ancestors.
>
> But unlike Europe, which remained fragmented after the collapse of the Romans, China was reunited in the 6th century with the establishment of the Sui Dynasty. Agricultural land and transportation options were expanded through the construction of hundreds of miles of **canals**. This allowed people to leave the more crowded areas of northern China and move south towards the Yangtze River.
>
> Following the Sui dynasty was the Tang dynasty (618-907) and the Song dynasty (960-1279). Together, these two dynasties make up another "golden age" of Chinese history. The **merit system** that was established during the Han dynasty was revived and the government structures were flooded with young men from affluent families. While still considered an autocracy with an emperor with immense power, the day-to-day workings of the government were organized under a variety of "ministries" or government offices.
>
> Chinese culture spread to other parts of Asia during this time. Korea, Vietnam, and Japan all interacted with the Chinese, whether through conflict, trade, or a combination of both. By the 13th century, Chinese influence was felt throughout east Asia. Ongoing conflicts with northern nomadic tribes would prove to be a greater challenge in the coming centuries, leading to the end of this golden era with the arrival of the Mongols in 1209.

**1.** Which dynasty reunified China in the 6th century CE?

**A.** Tang          **B.** Song          **C.** Qin          **D.** Sui

**2.** Which religion established a presence in China during the Sui dynasty?

**A.** Christianity      **B.** Islam          **C.** Hinduism      **D.** Buddhism

**3.** Which Han-era practice was revived during the Tang dynasty?

**A.** The merit system
**B.** Book burning
**C.** Legalism
**D.** Confucianism

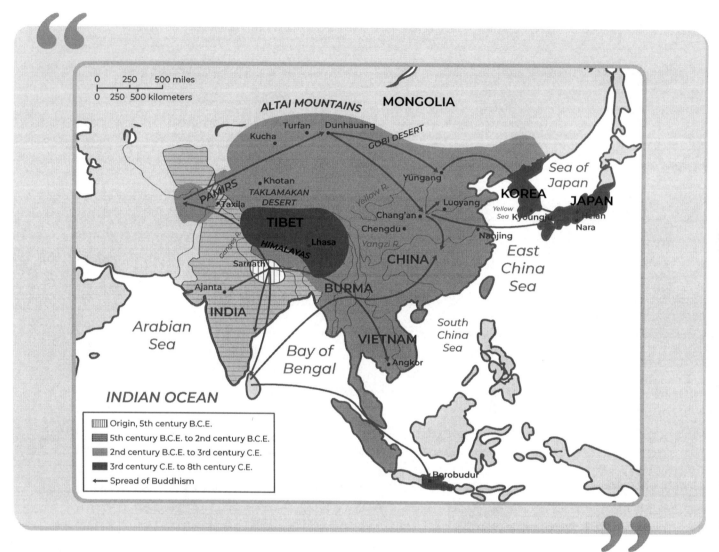

1. Where did Buddhism originate?

   **A.** Khotan          **B.** Sarnath          **C.** Angkor          **D.** Nanjing

2. Where did Buddhism first spread?

   **A.** Japan                          **C.** India
   **B.** Korea                          **D.** China

3. During which centuries did Buddhism spread the most throughout China?

   **A.** 5th - 2nd centuries BCE

   **B.** 2nd century BCE - 3rd century CE

   **C.** 3rd century CE - 8th century CE

   **D.** After the 8th century CE

**4.** The region labeled "Tibet" is geographically quite close to the origin of Buddhism. However, the map shows that it was one of the latest regions to adopt Buddhism. Use the map to determine why Buddhism spread more slowly to Tibet compared to the rest of east and south Asia.

..................................................................................................................................

..................................................................................................................................

..................................................................................................................................

..................................................................................................................................

..................................................................................................................................

..................................................................................................................................

..................................................................................................................................

**Directions:** Read the text below. Then answer the questions that follow.

One of the themes of history and geography is studying how groups of people interact. We often study how one group uses military tactics to take over another group, and it might seem that history is just one long chain of warfare. But there is another way that one group can exert control over another, and that is through the spread of culture.

In Tang and Song China, a specific method of interacting with the neighboring peoples of Korea, Vietnam, and Japan developed. China was unarguably the strongest and most advanced power in the region, and the Tang and Song emperors knew that. At times, bordering regions of Vietnam and Korea were under Chinese military control, but other times they remained independent. The leaders of the surrounding regions did not want to constantly be at war with the Chinese, while at the same time they wanted access to the luxuries that China produced. This led to an ongoing interaction known as the **tribute system**.

Representatives from the neighboring region would travel to the capital with "gifts" for the emperor. The tribute gifts would be presented to the emperor and the visitors would participate in a bowing ritual that acknowledged the emperor's superiority. Then the visitors were given gifts from the emperor - the most important of which was permission to travel within the region and trade with the rapidly-growing Chinese population. The other gifts they received would be returned to their region and used to establish their own power.

As a result of the tribute system, and continued interactions between neighboring groups, many elements of Chinese culture spread to Korea, Vietnam, and Japan. All three regions adopted elements of the Chinese writing system, government structure, Buddhism, and Confucianism. In most cases, the Chinese influence mixed with the local traditions to create unique cultures that had familiar elements of Chinese culture, but were distinctly Korean, or Vietnamese, or Japanese.

**1.** Describe the tribute system in your own words.

...................................................................................................................................

...................................................................................................................................

...................................................................................................................................

...................................................................................................................................

**2.** How was the tribute system able to maintain Chinese influence in the region without constant warfare?

...................................................................................................................................

...................................................................................................................................

...................................................................................................................................

...................................................................................................................................

**Directions:** Read the text below and follow the instructions to complete the activity.

One of the most practical inventions of the Tang and Song dynasties was the invention of paper money. Coins in China were made from different metals and had a hole in the middle so they could be carried on a string or rope. But that system was not convenient for long-distance trade and transactions that involved a high value. Merchants began to exchange coins for "flying cash" or "flying money," which was a certificate stating the value of coin that had been deposited. The merchant could then exchange the flying money for coin in the next town.

The Chinese government eventually adopted the system and established formal exchange centers. This led to more people using flying money. Eventually, the process evolved into printing paper money, which was accepted as currency and did not need to be converted back into coin.

1. Why was flying money useful to merchants?

........................................................................................................................................

........................................................................................................................................

2. How is Chinese "flying money" similar to the money system in the United States and other countries?

........................................................................................................................................

........................................................................................................................................

**Directions:** Read the text below and follow the instructions to complete the activity.

> As we have seen with other civilizations, "golden eras" often lead to advancements in science and technology. Some of the most significant inventions in world history emerged from China during the Tang and Song dynasties.
>
> An early form of **gunpowder** was developed, most likely by accident. It wasn't widely used in warfare until later, when small bags of gunpowder connected to a fuse were attached to an arrow. The fuse could be lit, the arrow launched from a bow or crossbow, and the arrow would be on fire by the time it hit its target. Bombs, fire lances, and other uses developed in the centuries that followed. Gunpowder would play an important part in warfare from the 14th century on.
>
> Another invention that would have long-lasting effects is the **magnetic compass**. While the knowledge of magnetic north had existed for some time, it was during Tang and Song dynasties that the pointer arrow was made smaller and placed in a hand-held device. The magnetic compass plus the astrolabe would have a direct effect on the global voyages that would begin in the 15th century.
>
> The Chinese established a presence in the South China Sea and Indian Ocean early on. In addition to navigation technology like the compass and astrolabe, another invention revolutionized sea travel. Using a **rudder** to steer a ship allowed for more precise navigation. Instead of relying on the placement of sails or the strength of the rowers, a rudder could be used to turn a ship more efficiently. This invention would increase the power of the Chinese navy in the following centuries.

**1.** The magnetic compass was used to find directions (north, east, south, and west). The astrolabe was used to determine how far north or south of the equator the user was located. Describe how the compass and the astrolabe could be used to navigate ships over long distances.

........................................................................................................................................

........................................................................................................................................

........................................................................................................................................

........................................................................................................................................

........................................................................................................................................

........................................................................................................................................

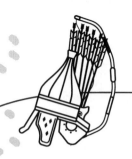

# The Mongols

This week you will learn about one of the great "exceptions" of history, the Mongols.

ARGOPREP

**Directions:** Read the text below. Then answer the questions that follow.

"

Historians, archaeologists, and anthropologists have worked together to study civilizations for many years. They have determined the major characteristics of a civilization (which we discussed in Weeks 3-5). All of the civilizations that have had a major impact on world history have shared similar characteristics, except for one group: The Mongols.

During the 13th and 14th centuries, this central Asian nomadic group managed to control much of Eurasia without the structures that other civilizations developed. After the often brutal conquering of established cities and empires, the Mongols maintained the largest land empire in world history.

The surprising success of the Mongols was based in part on centuries of living in the harsh land and climate of central Asia. The various Mongol tribes were nomadic pastoralists, moving with their herds throughout the seasons. They were accustomed to frequent movement, so they did not have much in the way of permanent settlements - they could quickly set up and take down their dwellings as movement was needed. This also meant that they were resourceful in keeping their communities supplied with food and resources without needing to rely on established cities. Both men and women were equally skilled in horseback riding and hunting with a compound bow. Horses were kept in abundance so Mongol riders always had a fresh mount available.

Around 1200 C.E., a Mongol leader named Temujin was determined to increase the strength of the Mongols by uniting the different tribes. In 1206 Temujin was recognized as the Great Khan, and became known as Genghis Khan. Genghis first moved against the Chinese dynasties in the south, most of whom were experiencing an era of political instability. The swift movement of Mongol forces as well as their ability to quickly adapt on the battlefield meant that the Chinese armies that relied on an organized response were quickly overrun.

After conquering most of China, the Mongols moved west into the middle east and eastern Europe. Cities that put up a resistance were wiped out and populations were slaughtered. Those that surrendered were mostly left intact. To the Muslim world especially, the Mongol conquests destroyed centuries of knowledge. The House of Wisdom in Baghdad, the center of Muslim learning for 800 years, was burnt down, and legend states that so many books were thrown into the Tigris that the river ran black with ink. The qanat irrigation systems of ancient Persia were filled in and collapsed, destroying settled agriculture for centuries.

By the 1220s, the Mongols had conquered most of the settled regions of Eurasia. Genghis Khan died in 1227 and the control of the Mongol territory was divided up amongst his generals. Over time, the Mongols that settled in each of the "Khanates,"

"

> or areas ruled by a Mongol Khan, adopted the languages, cultures, and religions of the areas they conquered. By the end of the 1300s, the Mongol Khanates were either conquered by other empires or culturally absorbed into local society.
>
> While on one hand the Mongol conquests led to the death of millions of people and the destruction of centuries of knowledge, it also led to the first long-lasting contacts between east and west. By establishing control of most of the ancient Silk Roads trade network, merchants and travelers were able to spread goods and information from eastern China to medieval Europe. The Indian number system spread through the Arab world and led to the numerical writing system (0, 1, 2, 3, etc.) that is used by billions of people today. Travelers such as Marco Polo and Ibn Battuta visited far away lands and brought their experiences home, leading to an increased awareness of other parts of the world. Knowledge of science, mathematics, and medicine spread throughout the networks that developed. For better or worse, the Mongol conquests had an enormous impact on world history.

**1.** The Mongols emerged from which region of Asia?

    **A.** Northern        **B.** Eastern        **C.** Southern        **D.** Central

**2.** The Mongols were highly skilled in which of the following?

    **A.** Horseback riding and archery        **C.** Agricultural techniques

    **B.** Smithing and metalwork        **D.** Infrastructure and public works

**3.** Which region was not conquered by the Mongols?

    **A.** China

    **B.** The Middle East

    **C.** North Africa

    **D.** Parts of Russia and Eastern Europe

**4.** The destruction of which of the following led to the loss of centuries of knowledge?

    **A.** The Library at Alexandria

    **B.** The Great Pyramid of Giza

    **C.** The House of Wisdom in Baghdad

    **D.** The Hanging Gardens of Babylon

**Directions:** Read the text below. Then answer the questions that follow.

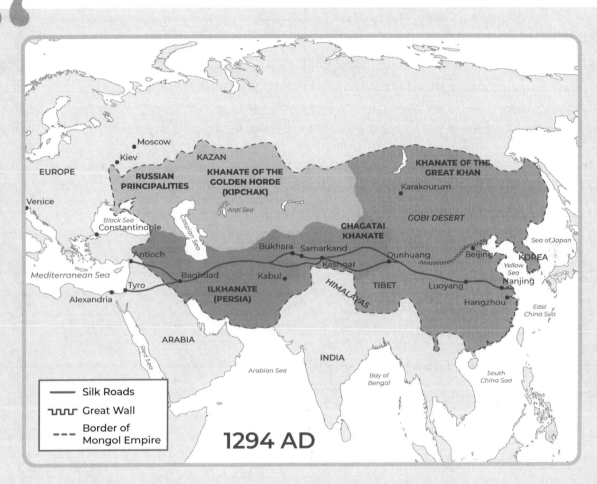

1294 AD

Legend:
— Silk Roads
ᴗᴗᴗ Great Wall
--- Border of Mongol Empire

Genghis Khan's empire was divided into four Khanates after his death: The Yuan Dynasty in China (Khanate of the Great Khan), the Chagatai Khanate in central Asia, the Ilkhanate in Persia and the Middle East, and the Khanate of the Golden Horde in Russia and parts of eastern Europe.

**1.** Which Khanate controlled the largest amount of territory?

   **A.** Khanate of the Great Khan

   **B.** Chagatai Khanate

   **C.** Ilkhanate

   **D.** Khanate of the Golden Horde

**2.** Which major city conquered by the Mongols was NOT located along the Silk Roads trade network?

   **A.** Samarkand            **C.** Karakorum

   **B.** Baghdad              **D.** Dunhuang

**3.** Which present-day Asian country is NOT in a region that was conquered by the Mongols? Look up a present-day map online to help you!

   **A.** Mongolia            **C.** Iraq

   **B.** Afghanistan        **D.** Japan

**4.** Using a present-day map of Eurasia, identify one country that exists at the farthest eastern border of the Mongol Empire, and one that exists at the furthest western border.

.................................................................................................................

.................................................................................................................

.................................................................................................................

.................................................................................................................

.................................................................................................................

.................................................................................................................

.................................................................................................................

**Directions:** Read the text below. Then answer the questions that follow.

> The success of the Mongol invasions is based on their mastery of two important skills: horseback riding and archery. And the combination of those two things during battle had an enormous effect on the Mongol's ability to move quickly, cause chaos and destruction within the enemy forces, and get out with speed and agility.
>
> The Mongol's skill with mounted archery was enhanced by the use of stirrups (which allowed the rider to have improved balance by using their legs to counter the movement of the horse) and the saddle (allowing them a brace to use when pulling back on their powerful bows.)
>
> The Mongols also used a compound bow. A compound bow is much more difficult to pull back, but can propel the arrow farther and with much more destructive force when it lands. The combination of skilled mounted archers with incredibly powerful bows was no match for many empires' reliance on ground forces armed with weaker bows and swords.

1. Ancient battles generally involved a large number of soldiers from one side marching towards a large number of soldiers from the opposing side. In the space below, write or draw how this type of battle might be different when met by the Mongols.

...................................................................................................................................................

...................................................................................................................................................

...................................................................................................................................................

...................................................................................................................................................

...................................................................................................................................................

...................................................................................................................................................

**Directions:** Read the text below. Then answer the question that follows.

One of the things that is most fascinating about the Mongols is how quickly the region went from invasions and massacres to an era marked by peace, increased long-distance trade, and a great devotion to the arts. The Mongols themselves did not create much in the way of a distinct art or architectural style, however they were great supporters of the arts in the regions they ruled. They were also highly tolerant of differing religious beliefs and promoted religious tolerance throughout the empire.

Prior to their Eurasian conquests, the Mongols had established a series of "rest stops" along important routes, which allowed Mongol messengers to rest, refuel, and obtain a fresh horse. This system continued and was enhanced along the existing Silk Roads trade network that the Mongols controlled. As a result, Silk Road trade became faster, safer, and more productive. It was said that a maiden holding a golden nugget on her outstretched hand could travel the length of the Silk Roads without being bothered. This exaggerated description is supported by the historical evidence of a Pax Mongolica, or "Mongol Peace." (Historians modeled this phrase after the Pax Romana, the Roman era of peace and economic prosperity from the 3rd to 5th centuries C.E.).

Imagine yourself as a merchant traveling along the Silk Roads. Along the way, you will meet people with languages, customs, and clothing that is very different from your own. Write a letter home that describes what it is like to meet people that are so different from yourself, and something that you might learn as a result of these interactions.

**Directions:** Read the text below. Add three more negative and positive effects of the Mongols in the table below. You can research online to help you learn more about the Mongols. Then answer the question that follows.

| Negative Effects of the Mongols | Positive Effects of the Mongols |
|---|---|
| * **Brutal & destructive** <br> * **Loss of valuable knowledge (library in Baghdad)** <br> * <br> * <br> * | * **Increased trade** <br> * **Religious tolerance** <br> * <br> * <br> * |

Historians continue to debate the role that the Mongols play in world history. Did the stability they brought to Eurasian trade outweigh the brutality they showed while taking over their territory? Does their support for the various cultures they lived in outweigh the destruction of the Baghdad House of Worship and other centers of knowledge and learning?

Using information from this week as well as your own research, construct an essay of at least two paragraphs that explores the positive as well as the negative effects of Mongol rule. Your essay should ultimately take a stand and state whether the Mongols had a positive or negative effect on history.

# WEEK 18

# Afro-Eurasian Land Trade

This week will focus on the interactions of multiple cultures through land-based trade: the Silk Roads in Asia and the Trans-Saharan trade routes in northern Africa.

ARGOPREP

# Afro-Eurasian Trade Routes
## ENGAGING WITH THE TOPIC

**Directions:** Read the text below. Then answer the questions that follow.

When studying world history, it is easy to think about the ancient world as a series of individual cultures that existed separate from each other. In reality, much of Afro-Eurasia has been interconnected through trade for thousands of years. Distant kingdoms were indirectly connected by a series of trade routes that spanned from the Mediterranean to eastern China, as well as from western Africa to the Mediterranean and Egypt. Regular contact connected the groups that lived along the Mediterranean coastline, and an important north-south trade network connected parts of Russia to the primarily east-west networks further south.

The two most influential long-distance trade routes of Afro-Eurasia were the Trans-Saharan network across northern Africa, and the Silk Roads network between eastern China and the Middle East. Both of these routes were made up of a series of interconnecting links, just like a chain. Merchants would travel back and forth along one "link" of the chain, interacting with other merchants at major trading centers where the "links" would intersect and goods would be bought and sold (and information shared). Merchants would then return to the previous trading center to trade what they had received for more goods (and share information). This back-and-forth was repeated all along these vast trading networks. While a few individuals did travel great lengths and brought back stories of distant lands, merchants primarily focused on their own "link" of the network.

In addition to goods that were exchanged along these trade routes, there was also a transfer of information. Technological advancements were shared as merchants interacted with each other. Languages were learned (and created) to facilitate trade. Religions grew and spread as certain groups gave preferential treatment to those of a particular belief system. These interactions also had unintended consequences: the spread of diseases. As merchants met and interacted, there was also an exchange of bacteria and viruses. The most famous was the Black Death, which spread all along the existing trade networks and led to millions of deaths throughout Afro-Eurasia in the 13th and 14th centuries.

Another important effect of the trade routes was the spread of religion. Buddhism spread west from China into parts of central Asia. Buddhist shrines were built along caravan routes and can still be seen today. Islam quickly spread due to the success of Muslim armies, but it continued to spread along trade routes. Islam moved from the north coast of Africa south to the empires of Mali, Ghana, and Songhai. It also spread into India due to Mongol control (the Mughal Empire) who had previously converted to Islam. Christianity also had a presence, primarily along the Silk Roads, but at this time it was not as widespread as Islam and Buddhism.

**1.** Merchants along the trade routes would primarily
   **A.** Travel the entire distance
   **B.** Travel back-and-forth between 2-3 major trade centers
   **C.** Frequently cross the Trans-Saharan route before starting the Silk Roads route
   **D.** Focus on staying in one city throughout the year.

**2.** Which of the following was generally NOT exchanged along the trade routes?
   **A.** Religions               **C.** Perishable foods
   **B.** Languages               **D.** Goods

**3.** Which disease spread along the trade networks in the 13th and 14th centuries and led to the death of millions of people in Afro-Eurasia?
   **A.** The Black Death         **C.** Malaria
   **B.** Smallpox                **D.** Ebola

**4.** What type of information might be shared from merchant to merchant and end up traveling across incredibly long distances?
   **A.** Local gossip
   **B.** News of the wedding of a local noble
   **C.** A significant weather event
   **D.** A major technological breakthrough

**Directions:** Read the text below. Then answer the questions that follow.

Named after the textile that was China's most valuable secret for centuries, the Silk Roads were a series of trade routes that traveled from eastern China to the eastern shore of the Mediterranean Sea. While trade along the Silk Roads peaked under Mongol rule in the 14th century, there is evidence of east-west trade for at least 2000 years prior. There are multiple references to the desirability of silk among Roman nobles. Buddhist statues in China have been found that are wearing Greek-style robes. And across the entire continent can be found references to the ever-expensive spices.

With the exception of the Mongol period, the regions through which the Silk Roads crossed were controlled by various groups. Each local leader wanted to profit from the trade that moved through their land, so merchants were often heavily taxed. These taxes were passed on to consumers, making trade along the Silk Road very expensive. As a result, the goods that moved along the Silk Roads were primarily luxury goods. Silk, of course, along with delicate porcelain from China were popular. Spices and resins (scented tree sap used in incense) were traded in both directions. Europe contributed glassware, furs and honey. Essential goods were also traded, but they generally moved only short distances.

Long caravans of camels and horses would travel together for safety. Some routes passed through dangerous mountain passes, or around the edges of vast deserts. Some trading centers became powerful cities as were the first or last point before a dangerous stage. These cities, and the leaders who controlled them, became wealthy and powerful.

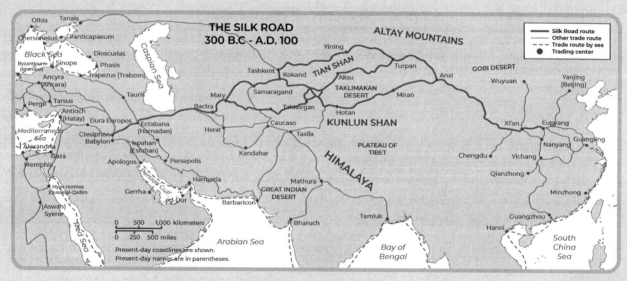

**1.** Other than silk, what was a major Chinese product that was traded along the Silk Roads?

   **A.** Spices     **B.** Horses     **C.** Camels     **D.** Porcelain

**2.** Which of the following is evidence of east-west trade during Roman times?

   **A.** A Roman noble using silk cloth as shade for guests

   **B.** A Persian merchant selling spices

   **C.** A Chinese merchant selling silk

   **D.** A Mongol merchant traveling with a group of horses

**3.** How did the Mongol period differ from other times in Silk Road history?

   **A.** Trade ceased completely     **C.** Only essential goods were traded

   **B.** The regions were not controlled by various groups     **D.** Taxes were higher than ever before

**4.** In your own words, describe why Silk Road merchants primarily traded expensive luxury goods.

.............................................................................................................................

.............................................................................................................................

.............................................................................................................................

.............................................................................................................................

**Directions:** Read the text below. Then answer the questions that follow.

The Trans-Saharan network was a series of trade routes that connected the western and sub-Saharan empires with the vast markets of the Mediterranean and the middle east. Massive camel caravans crossed the Sahara Desert carrying valuable goods. The camel caravans were supported by a series of oases that provided an opportunity to rest and refuel.

In addition to moving goods from the Mediterranean and middle eastern markets (including access to Silk Roads goods), the Trans-Saharan route was a major source of salt, gold, and slaves. Salt was difficult to obtain and it was used as a flavor enhancer as well as a method of food preservation, so it was incredibly valuable. Gold has been prized for centuries due to its malleability and luster. The selling of enslaved persons from conquered regions was also practiced. This combination made the empires of west and sub-Saharan Africa wealthy and powerful.

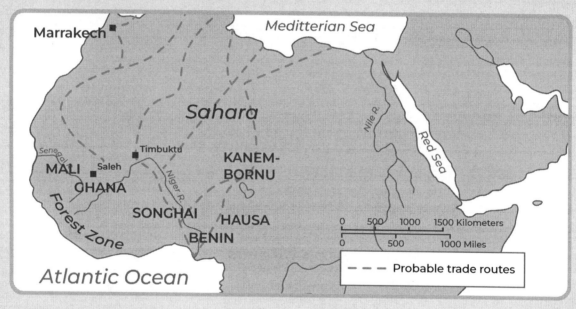

1. What skills do you think would be important to successfully trade along the Trans-Saharan routes?

.......................................................................................................

.......................................................................................................

.......................................................................................................

.......................................................................................................

**2.** You have learned that much of north Africa converted to Islam. You have also learned that Muslims are expected to take a pilgrimage to Mecca at least once in their life (the hajj). What do you think the effects of the hajj had on travel and trade in predominantly-Muslim areas?

.................................................................................................................................

.................................................................................................................................

.................................................................................................................................

.................................................................................................................................

.................................................................................................................................

.................................................................................................................................

.................................................................................................................................

.................................................................................................................................

.................................................................................................................................

**Directions:** Read the text below. Follow the instructions to complete the activity.

In the chart below you will read about three famous long-distance travelers who moved along the Afro-Eurasian trade routes.

### Ibn Battuta - 14th century, from Tangier in present-day Morocco

In an era before rapid transportation, Ibn Battuta traveled the entirety of the known world at the time. Originally planned as a pilgrimage to Mecca, a trip of many months, it turned into a nearly 30-year exploration of north Africa, the Middle East, Constantinople, east Africa, Persia, India, and China, with many diversions along the way. His education and intellect gained him the respect of many leaders and he served as an advisor to many rulers across Afro-Eurasia.

### Marco Polo - 13th century, from Venice in present-day Italy

Marco Polo was inspired by his father and uncle to travel to the court of Kublai Khan, the Mongol ruler of the Yuan Dynasty in China. Impressed with Polo's intelligence, the Khan named him an official representative and he traveled throughout the Mongol-controlled lands. He was the first European to record his experiences in China and his books became bestsellers and influenced many - including Christopher Columbus.

### Mansa Musa - 14th century, from present-day Mali

Mansa Musa also made a pilgrimage to Mecca. He was the king of the Mali Empire and traveled with a vast amount of gold mined from lands under his control. While passing through Egypt, it is said that he spent and gave away so much gold that the value of it dropped for nearly a decade. Prior to Mansa Musa's travels, the kingdom of Mali was barely known - after he returned from Mecca it became a center of culture and learning, especially the city of Timbuktu.

1. Do an internet search on the travels of Ibn Battuta. On the map below, label the route he took. Choose at least five places he lived and write a brief description of what he did there.

**Directions:** Read the text below. Then answer the questions that follow.

This week you have learned about the land-based trade routes of Afro-Eurasia. Different regions provided unique goods that were then traded over long distances in exchange for other goods.

For each region in the chart below, use the internet or a world history text to identify additional goods that were produced and traded along the Trans-Sahara and/or Silk Roads. Try to find at least three additional products for each region.

| Africa | Middle East | China |
|---|---|---|
| * **Salt** | * **Resins (find specific examples)** | * **Silk** |
| * **Gold** | | * **Porcelain** |
| * **Slaves** | * **Spices (find specific examples)** | * |
| * | | * |
| * | * | * |
| * | * | * |
| | * | |

# WEEK 19

# Indian Ocean Trade

This week will focus on the interactions of multiple cultures through ocean-based trade along the Indian Ocean trade network. Communities thousands of miles apart were able to interact due to knowledge of the ocean wind currents.

ARGOPREP

**Directions:** Read the text below. Then answer the questions that follow.

The Indian Ocean is the third-largest ocean in the world. The present-day country of India juts into it, and it is bordered on the west by the east coast of Africa, and on the east by northwest Australia and the islands of present-day Indonesia. For those in south Asia and along the shores of the Indian Ocean, life is dictated by the monsoon. The pattern of warm, moist air coming from the ocean alternating with cool, dry air from the Himalayas creates a seasonal wind cycle. Sailors have been using this predictable cycle for thousands of years. As knowledge of the monsoon spread, and advancements in naval technology developed, a complex trading network developed in the Indian Ocean.

By using the direction of the seasonal monsoon winds, merchants from India and Arabia could sail to the east coast of Africa and return during the next monsoon season. East African merchants would do the same. A similar pattern developed on the eastern side of India, allowing merchants to sail to and from the islands of present-day Indonesia.

This consistent pattern allowed for centuries of contact between groups of people who were separated by thousands of miles of open ocean, but due to the monsoon winds could expect to have yearly contact with each other.

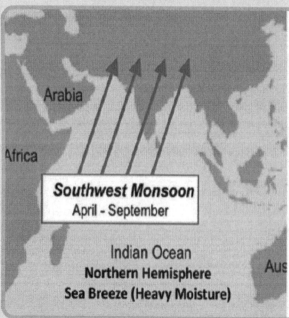
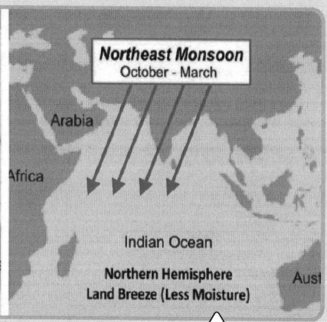

1. The monsoon is caused by

   A. Flooding in higher elevations

   B. The interaction between warm, moist air and cool, dry air

   C. Ocean currents between Europe and west Africa

   D. The atmospheric jet stream over Asia

2. Merchants from which two regions made use of the monsoon winds?

   A. North Africa and southern Europe

   B. East Asia and Central Asia

   C. North Africa and Sub-Saharan Africa

   D. South Asia and East Africa

3. From April to September, people in South Asia can expect to feel which type of weather?

   A. Hot and wet                    C. Cool and wet

   B. Cool and dry                   D. Hot and dry

4. In which of the following months would a merchant from Arabia want to leave to reach east Africa?

   A. December

   B. May

   C. July

   D. September

**Directions:** Read the text below. Then answer the questions that follow.

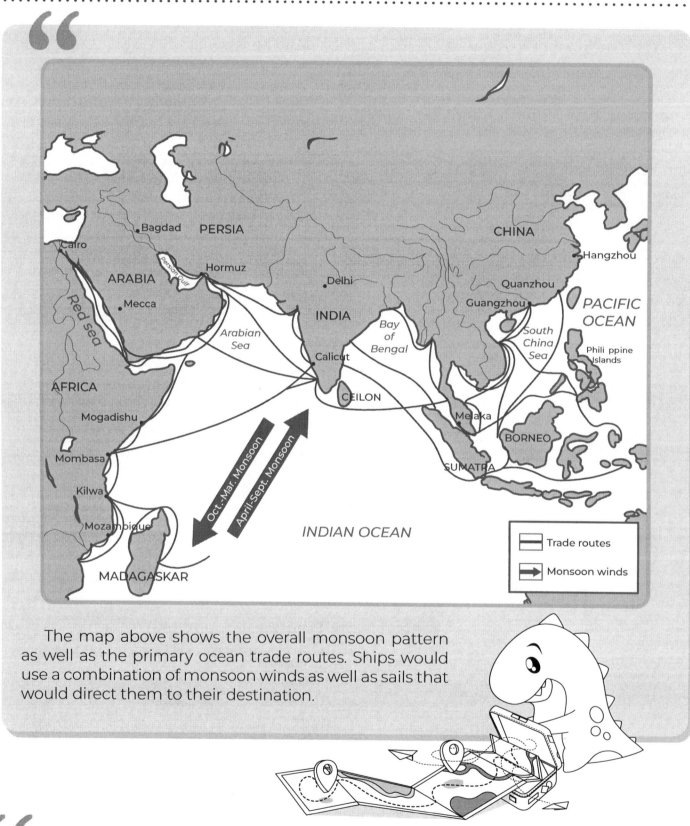

The map above shows the overall monsoon pattern as well as the primary ocean trade routes. Ships would use a combination of monsoon winds as well as sails that would direct them to their destination.

1. Which city would be a logical connection between the Indian Ocean network and the Silk Roads network?

   A. Cairo

   B. Hormuz

   C. Delhi

   D. Mogadishu

2. Which city would be a likely connection between the Indian Ocean network and the Trans-Saharan network?

   A. Baghdad

   B. Mombasa

   C. Calicut

   D. Cairo

3. Someone sailing from Quanzhou to Melaka would sail through which body of water?

   A. Indian Ocean

   B. Bay of Bengal

   C. South China Sea

   D. Arabian Sea

4. A person who wanted to sail from Kilwa to Calicut would likely leave during which month?

   A. July

   B. October

   C. December

   D. March

**Directions:** Read the text below. Follow the instructions to complete the activity.

"

A gigantic and ferocious bird guarded the cinnamon sticks used to build its nest, and it was only by luring the bird away with a piece of meat could the hunter retrieve the valuable spice...

The mythical origins of cinnamon were much more interesting than the reality: The dried inner bark of the cinnamon tree. But a story like this served multiple purposes - Not only did it drive the cost of cinnamon higher, it helped keep its origin secret.

Throughout the history of the eastern hemisphere, spices have been some of the most valued substances. For a time, black peppercorn, the same pepper that comes ground in little packets at restaurants, was worth more than gold. Many of the spices we use today were originally cultivated in south and southeast Asia. Present-day Indonesia, Malaysia, Myanmar, India, and Sri Lanka were some of the ancient origins of popular spices. Further east are the islands of Maluku and the Bandas. These islands were the only source of spices such as nutmeg and cloves. The combination of distant lands, mythological origins, and expensive shipping methods kept prices high. But today, many spices have become staples of kitchen cupboards and their mythological origins have been long forgotten.

"

Choose four spices from your kitchen or the spice aisle at the grocery store. Use the internet to look up where the spice is produced today, where it was originally produced, and one or two examples of how that spice can be used.

| Spice | Historical Origin | Current Origin | Uses |
|---|---|---|---|
|  |  |  |  |
|  |  |  |  |
|  |  |  |  |
|  |  |  |  |

**Directions:** Read the text below. Follow the instructions to complete the activity.

Technological developments allowed Indian Ocean sailors to more quickly and safely navigate the waters. Three of the most important technologies were the **astrolabe, junk ship, dhow ship and lateen sail**.

### The Astrolabe

Used in conjunction with the **compass**, the astrolabe helps determine at which latitude a ship is sailing. Knowing the latitude and the direction allows sailors to make adjustments to their course and ensure a more accurate destination.

### Junk

The junk ship, still in use today, was a shallow-bottomed ship that could sail in shallow waters. It had battened sails, which meant that the sails were reinforced with bamboo for stability in high winds. The junk also had a rudder, allowing the ship to be steered and not fully relying on the wind. These ships could hold a large amount of cargo.

### Dhow ship with lateen sail

These have been in use for thousands of years, and are still used today. The lateen sail can be raised and lowered, and its triangular shape allows for small adjustments to catch even the lightest winds. The dhow can be made in a variety of sizes, and all of them can support heavy cargo.

### Admiral Zheng He

Born to a Chinese Muslim family in the late 1300s, Zheng He became one of China's greatest naval admirals. Zheng He served at the court of the Ming emperor and sailed throughout the Indian Ocean to show the power of the Chinese. He made multiple voyages around the region, venturing as far as the southern Swahili coastline of east Africa, Persia, and the islands of present-day Indonesia. He also completed the hajj by reaching Mecca. Zheng He's voyages are considered the beginning of an era of Chinese influence in the Indian Ocean.

Choose one of the topics above. Use the internet or a history text to learn more about the topic you've chosen. In the space below, write three additional things you have learned as a result of your research.

.................................................................................................................................

.................................................................................................................................

.................................................................................................................................

.................................................................................................................................

.................................................................................................................................

.................................................................................................................................

.................................................................................................................................

.................................................................................................................................

.................................................................................................................................

.................................................................................................................................

**Directions:** Read the text below. Follow the instructions to complete the activity.

> One of the best examples of the interconnectedness of the Indian Ocean is the east coast of Africa. Known as the **Swahili** coast, this region is the product of centuries of African, Arab, and Indian interactions. Cities devoted to Indian Ocean trade developed. Some of the most important were Mogadishu, Mombasa, Zanzibar, and Kilwa. These cities housed merchants from all over the Indian Ocean trade network and led to an incredible amount of cultural interaction. Since the monsoon winds shifted direction twice a year, merchants who sailed from Arabia or India would remain along the Swahili coast for nearly half a year before the winds allowed them to return home. The same would happen for Swahili merchants who sailed to Arabia or India. These interactions over time led to a distinct culture and language.
>
> The term syncretism refers to a new characteristic that is created when two or more cultures mix. The new characteristic is unique, but traces of the original characteristics can still be seen. The Swahili language is an example of a syncretic language. It is a combination of indigenous east African Bantu and Arabic. Centuries of trade between Arabia and east Africa led to the development of this distinct language. Swahili is still spoken in the region today, and is the official language of many east African countries.
>
> Arab merchants spread Islam along with trade goods. The people of the Swahili coastline adopted Islam early on, and the region's connection to Arabia was reinforced each season as Muslim merchants awaited the next season's monsoons. Today, the people along the Swahili coastline consider themselves part of a larger ethnic group, one that is distinct from African or Arab.

**Directions:** Respond to one of the two prompts below:

**A.** Think about a time you were interacting with a person who spoke a different language. How did you communicate? Did you create any words or gestures to provide meaning? Imagine that you were isolated with speakers of another language for many years. How do you think your language might change?

**B.** You have probably experienced that the language you use as a young person is different from the language an older person uses, even if you technically speak the same language. Describe an occasion where you were speaking with someone from an older generation. What terms did they use that you didn't know? Were there any words they used that embarrassed you? What words did you use that were unfamiliar to the other person? If you were isolated with a group of people from an older generation for many years, how do you think your language might change?

# WEEK 20

# Oceania & Polynesian Migrations

This week you will learn about the geography and navigational technology of the interconnected island networks of the Pacific Ocean.

ARGOPREP

**Directions:** Read the text below. Then answer the questions that follow.

The vast Pacific Ocean covers nearly one-third of the Earth's surface. Human settlement along its coastlines dates back thousands of years. But the island chains within its southern waters are more recently inhabited.

Historians believe that the first people to travel to the South Pacific came from east and southeast Asia over 5000 years ago. Groups "island hopped," by establishing settlements on islands, and then later groups continued on to nearby islands. Over time, human settlement stretched from the present-day Philippines to the northern coast of New Guinea. Eventually, these early settlers left behind the shorelines and ventured into the vast open ocean of the Pacific.

The navigation of the open ocean continues to be one of the world's most amazing accomplishments. Polynesians tracked the movements of the stars and other celestial bodies to maintain a course. They relied upon knowledge of the movement of ocean currents over different types of oceanic landforms. Even the patterns of bird flights could indicate the presence of a habitable island in the distance. This knowledge was passed down through generations in songs, stories, and artistic creations.

By the 9th century B.C.E., eastward migration seems to have stalled. Genetic and archaeological evidence shows that there was continued contact between previously settled islands, but that there was a thousand-year break before large-scale movements began again.

Another wave of migrations began in the 8th century C.E. Sailing in open canoes and relying on ancient wisdom, voyagers set out from the present-day islands of Samoa and established settlements as far north as Hawai'i, east to Te Henua 'Enana/ Te Fenua 'Enata (Marquesas Islands) and further east to Rapa Nui (Easter Island) and by the 1200s to Aotearoa (New Zealand).

**1.** Approximately how many years ago did Polynesians settle in Aotearoa/New Zealand?

**A.** 800          **B.** 1200          **C.** 1500          **D.** 3000

**2.** Polynesians passed down their seafaring knowledge through

**A.** Written texts                    **C.** Songs and stories

**B.** Stone carvings                   **D.** Construction of scale models

**3.** Once a region was settled, there was not very much back-and-forth interaction between islands.

**A.** True          **B.** False

**Directions:** Read the text below. Then answer the questions that follow.

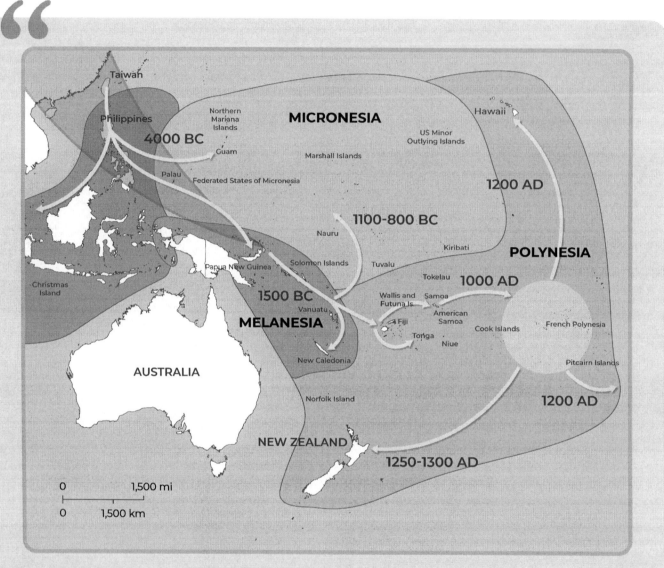

The islands of the Pacific Ocean are loosely divided into three major groups. Most of the earliest settlement was in Melanesia, the region closest to New Guinea, which includes the present-day countries of Vanuatu and Fiji. To the north of Melanesia is Micronesia. The Federated States of Micronesia and the Marshall Islands are found in Micronesia. To the east and north is Polynesia, which includes Samoa, Aotearoa, Rapa Nui, and Hawai'i.

**1.** Samoa is approximately how many miles from New Guinea?

   **A.** 3000 miles        **C.** 1000 miles

   **B.** 4500 miles        **D.** 500 miles

**2.** What is the approximate distance between Fiji and Vanuatu?

   **A.** 500 miles        **C.** 2,000 miles

   **B.** 1500 miles        **D.** 2500 miles

**3.** Which of the following is NOT a collection of islands in the Pacific?

   **A.** Madagascar

   **B.** Micronesia

   **C.** Melanesia

   **D.** Polynesia

**Directions:** Read the text below. Then answer the questions that follow.

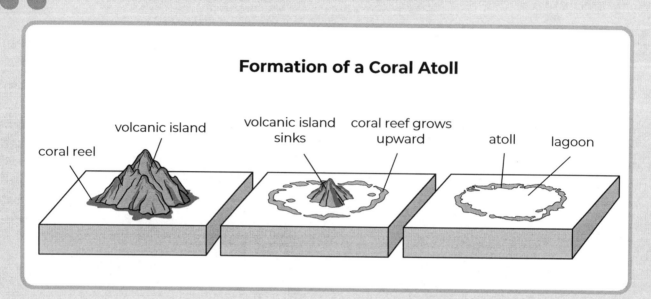

**Formation of a Coral Atoll**

The people living on the islands of the Pacific Ocean have adapted to extreme conditions. The majority of people live on one of three main types of islands: continental islands, volcanic islands, and coral atolls.

* **Continental islands were formed by the earth's crust rising above the level of the ocean. These islands are generally found closer to other large land masses. New Guinea and New Zealand are examples of continental islands.**

* **Volcanic islands are formed over a "hot spot" or weak area in the earth's crust. Magma pushes up through the weak area to become lava, which then cools and creates volcanic rock. An island is formed as the hardened lava builds up and emerges above the surface of the ocean. The Hawaiian islands are examples of volcanic islands.**

* **Atolls are the land left behind after a volcanic island sinks back into the sea. Coral reefs develop around volcanic islands. The reefs continue to grow in size around the base of the island. Eventually, the volcanic island erodes or sinks back into the sea, leaving behind a ring of coral.**

This ring of coral now surrounds a lagoon and is usually of very low elevation. Atolls can be found all throughout the region.

**1.** Enewetak is one of the islands in the Marshall Islands. Enewetak surrounds a lagoon and has an average elevation of 16 feet above sea level. Which type of island is Enewetak?

   **A.** Continental

   **B.** Atoll

   **C.** Volcanic

**2.** In September 2022, a new island emerged from the ocean due to lava build-up from an underwater eruption. This new island would be classified as which type?

   **A.** Continental

   **B.** Atoll

   **C.** Volcanic

**3.** Most atolls are only a handful of yards in elevation, and often less than a mile in width. Which of the following issues are very important to inhabitants of atolls?

   **A.** Rising sea levels

   **B.** Contamination of freshwater by seawater

   **C.** Flooding

   **D.** All of the above

**Directions:** Read the text below. Then complete the activity that follows.

"

The canoes used by Polynesian voyagers were made from the natural materials available on individual islands, so while the styles might be similar, the materials are varied. For shorter ventures and for those remaining closer to shore, single-hulled canoes with a stabilizing float off to the side were used. Longer voyages incorporated multiple sails and sometimes had two hulls for greater durability.

The triangular sails were used to take advantage of even the slightest breeze. Even if the air was not moving in the desired direction, the angle of the sail could be adjusted to catch the wind. A large paddle would be used to adjust for the desired direction.

"

**1.** Describe some of the challenges that Polynesian sailors would need to overcome while on the open ocean.

..................................................................................................................................................

..................................................................................................................................................

..................................................................................................................................................

..................................................................................................................................................

**2.** Imagine you were on one of these canoes, and you did not know how long you would be sailing. What would you do to keep yourself occupied and motivated?

..................................................................................................................................................

..................................................................................................................................................

..................................................................................................................................................

..................................................................................................................................................

..................................................................................................................................................

**Directions:** Read the text below. Then answer the questions that follow.

Polynesian sailors developed many tools to help with navigation. Two of the tools used by Polynesian sailors were the stick chart and the star compass.

Stick charts were used as a tool to provide a visualization for the location of ocean currents and the direction of waves as the water came upon different islands. In this stick chart above, the islands are marked by shells, and the sticks and wrappings around the sticks indicated the direction of the currents and wave shapes.

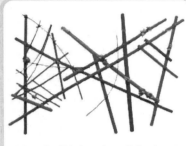

**Marshall Islands stick chart**

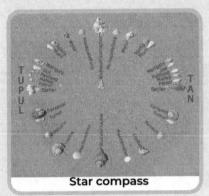

**Star compass**

The star compass was another way to visualize location and direction. Generally, the center represented the location of the canoe. A voyager would have memorized all of the brightest stars along the chart and used that knowledge to turn the desired direction. This would allow a navigator to maintain course at night, and could also be used based on the location of the sunrise and sunset.

**1.** How do these tools compare to navigation tools you may have used in the past?

........................................................................................................................

........................................................................................................................

**2.** In your opinion, is the stick chart more like a map or a compass? Explain your reasoning.

........................................................................................................................

........................................................................................................................

**3.** Do you feel it is important for people today to continue to learn how to use these tools, even though current technology means they are no longer necessary for navigation? Explain your answer.

........................................................................................................................

........................................................................................................................

........................................................................................................................

# Answer Sheets

To see the answer key to the entire workbook, you can easily download the answer key from our website!

*Due to the high request from parents and teachers, we have removed the answer key from the workbook so you do not need to rip out the answer key while students work on the workbook.

To watch free video explanations go to: **argoprep.com/social6**
OR scan the QR Code:

**Place your mouse over the workbook you have, and you will see the "Download Answers" button.**

**For detailed video instructions on how to access the "Answer Sheets," please scan this QR code.**

# Books explanations

 All Books     Grade: **All** ⌄     Series: **Social Studies** ⌄     🔍 Search...

7th Grade Social Studies: Daily Practice Workbook

5th Grade Social Studies: Daily Practice Workbook

8th Grade Social Studies: Daily Practice Workbook

4th Grade Social Studies: Daily Practice Workbook

3rd Grade Social Studies: Daily Practice Workbook

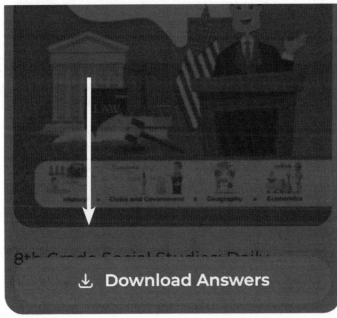

⬇ Download Answers

4th Grade Social Studies: Practice Workbook

Made in the USA
Middletown, DE
24 August 2024

59656982R00117